Black Power
Gary Style

Black Power Gary Style

The Making of Mayor Richard Gordon Hatcher

By

ALEX POINSETT

Johnson Publishing Company, Inc.
Chicago, 1970

Library of Congress Catalog Card No. 70–128547
SBN No. 87485–042–8
Printed in the United States of America
First edition, November, 1970

Design by Norman L. Hunter

To Norma
  Pierrette
    and Pierre
who also made
  the journey

Contents

Black Power Gary Style

IN SEPTEMBER, 1969, the Metropolitan Applied Research Center sponsored a three-day Institute for Black Elected Officials in Washington, D.C. Several hundred black elected office-holders—from local school board members and justices of the peace to mayors and state legislators and national congressmen—attended the meeting. Mayor Richard G. Hatcher of Gary, Indiana addressed the group in one of its plenary sessions. The tone, emphasis and direction of his thinking were set by his opening sentences:

> I have been asked to speak on the subject of the Negro in politics. Most of you realize by its very title, this speech is outdated. Because today there is no place for a *Negro* in politics.

What he meant, very clearly, was that *Negro* politics had certain implications which he felt no longer coincided with the demands of a new political day. This is a day that had its dawning in the post-World War II legal struggles of the NAACP, in the mass, southern protests of Dr. Martin Luther King Jr., in the direct action sit-in movement of the black college students, and in the new sociopolitical awareness of large numbers of black people in the northern urban ghettos. This new day meant that those black politicians who would strive for elective office would be required to have an orienta-

tion different from their predecessors who were described by
Professor Harold F. Gosnell in 1935 in his classic book, *Negro
Politicians: The Rise of Negro Politics in Chicago*. In an Introduction to that book, Professor Robert E. Park described
the Negro politicians who came into office in the 1920s and
1930s as men who no longer considered themselves as "wards
of the Republican Party." Rather, they adopted the attitude
of individualism, and were more identified with the philos-
ophy of Booker T. Washington and the Negro Business
League. In distinguishing them from the post-Civil War
politicians, Park wrote:

> The Negro politicians who have risen in ward politics, as dis-
> tinguished from those who still take their cue from Washing-
> ton [D.C.], seem to be, in most every case, of this type. They
> are not infrequently men of superior education and are active
> in promoting the interests of the race as they see them, but
> they act on the principle that the best way to solve the prob-
> lem of the race as a whole is for each member to solve the
> problem as an individual.

Mayor Hatcher represents still a newer type of black politician, one who recognizes the necessity not to be irrevocably
tied to an entrenched local political party, and at the same
time who knows that the ethic of individualism must yield
to a more collectivist notion of racial advancement.

Alex Poinsett's book clearly shows the development of
Mayor Hatcher as a new breed of black politician actor, as one
in tune with the times and with the new demands. Unlike
many of the earlier Negro politicians of the post-Civil War
and early twentieth century periods, Hatcher did not come
from a "colored aristocracy within the Negro race." He came
from a southern migrant family that "dreamed of owning a
home across town in East Port." He came from a family where,
in order to help finance his college education, his "sisters

Collie Bell and Gladys—'Man, they were beautiful'—started taking money out of their grocery allowances for his expenses." Hatcher is a product of the black struggle. His career is an example of the Black Experience, the Black Culture, of the dreams black lower-class parents have for their children. Those parents and siblings scraped and saved and sacrificed—and they dreamed. Out of such circumstances, it would be difficult for a Richard Hatcher to believe that he could "make it" on the sweat of his efforts *alone*. He must be influenced not by an ethic of individualism, but by a more communally oriented ethic that instilled in him a sense of group responsibility.

It would, in fact, be a betrayal of his heritage if Hatcher, now in office, assumed that he obtained that position without the long, historical, *collective* efforts of family, friends, and a substantial portion of the black community. The implications of this are many, but certainly one implication is that the new black politicians coming into office cannot be merely replacements for white politicians who have ruled so neglectfully and so racistly for so long. The new black office-holders represent a step—by no means final—on a long road toward equitable political power for a group in this country whose political experience is unique. Black Americans are the only citizens in the history of this land who have had to suffer death and decades of official delaying tactics merely to gain the *constitutional* right to vote! If the men the black voters successfully elected in a long process to overcome that despicable past proceeded to act in ways that did not take cognizance of the meaning of that historical struggle, they would be as anachronistic as the men they succeeded. The intense crisis-laden, survival-oriented nature of the black political struggle characterizes much of the black political culture. This is one important phenomenon that Poinsett has captured in this important account of black power Gary style. And this is a phenomenon too frequently overlooked by those attempting to study and to understand the new black people moving into the political arena today.

This helps to explain the context of Hatcher's opening statement to his fellow black elected officials, and this is why he could also say to them:

> . . . he [the black leader] must also tend to an absolutely crucial problem, particular to his own people, his black brothers and sisters: the development of a healthy vital black nationalism and black culture. . . . I am not talking about a black nationalism that is racist and reactionary, nationalism that seals off black society from the rest of the nation; that glories in separatism. . . . I am talking about a black nationalism that encourages, develops, subsidizes, and pays attention to its own culture, that takes pride in its color and its past, that rids itself of self-hate and self-doubt, that does not mirror and ape white society, especially the worst of it. . . . blacks must continue to organize themselves as blacks. In unions, in bar associations, among doctors—yes, even in politics; no, especially in politics—and that includes each and every one of us here today, no matter what the political party—*we must organize black!* When we gain strength and unity, we shall from time to time, as situations arise, and when we can be no less than equal partners and not dilute our historically just demands, ally ourselves on specific issues with nonblack groups who share our purposes and commitment.

Herein lies much of the essence of the dynamism of black power as it is being worked out and tried out in Gary, Indiana today. But there is more, as Poinsett's book describes. One hears language today of several dichotomies: reform versus revolution; working within the system versus co-optation, which is being consumed by the system; militant versus moderate. More frequently than not, this language and these discussions are conducted in abstract, theoretical contexts. But the Richard Hatchers of our time cannot afford such luxurious dialogs. They must go to their offices every day and try to work out daily, vexing problems. And if any one knows the relevancy of what Dr. W. E. B. Du Bois once said in 1917 about black activists—"We face a condition, not a theory"—it surely must be the Richard Hatchers of our society.

Hatcher is mayor of a city where, in the presidential primary of 1964, one census tract of white, working-class homeowners voted 77 percent for George Wallace, and where, overall, more than two-thirds of Gary's whites voted for the Alabama Governor. Any mayor—black or white—has to be aware of this, not for purposes of catering to the same instincts that found a Wallace candidacy appealing, but precisely because those statistics tell a great deal about the political orientation of a large number of citizens of the town who must be included in the body politic and who must be governed.

At the same time, Hatcher is mayor of a city whose black population is no longer willing to be governed by forces inattentive and nonresponsive to their just and fundamental needs. More than 90 percent of his vote in 1967 came from the black electorate. Thousands of whites, who traditionally voted for the Democratic candidate, switched to the Republican candidate.

His election was no panacea; it was, at best, only the beginning of a new political struggle. It was the beginning of a struggle to bring about meaningful changes before mutual racial hostility made changes impossible. There is a school of thought that says that the election of Richard Hatcher could only lead to co-optation of the black struggle. Electoral politics, the argument goes, at best, is reformist politics, and does not deal with the fundamental problems of power and oppression in the society. Black mayors, no less than white mayors, the doubtful assert, are, in the final analysis, victims of—if not partners in—an oppressive *status quo* power structure.

And this means that such mayors simply are not going to use their office and powers in any way which would seriously challenge that *status quo*. Hatcher is not unaware of these skeptical attitudes. In his September, 1969 speech, he said:

> Black political power is essential, but in and of itself, it is not enough. The black movement must more and more doggedly direct its thoughts and energies to the problems of economic power. And by economic power, I don't mean black capitalism, which is a travesty and a hoax. Since black people of this nation are, as a whole, the most deprived and oppressed, it must be black people who are the vanguard of the movement which demands that the system be radically transformed. . . .
>
> We cannot live, work, and struggle in the abstract. All struggle must center around current concrete problems. We must constantly demand these reforms and a host of others. But if all we do is attend to reforms, then we are only pallid reformers, dispensers of Mercurochrome and Band-Aids when nothing short of surgery is required. . . . How do we avoid the ancient pitfalls of working for reforms without at the same time becoming helpless reformers, errand boys of corporate liberalism, Uncle Thomases, if you will? We do so by not viewing the reforms themselves as ultimate goals, but by viewing the struggle around reforms as a means of radicalizing people's consciousness. . . .
>
> We don't abandon to George Wallace the white working class; they are fearful, confused, battered by inflation, barely making their mortgage payments. We point out to them the real enemy. We explain to them patiently, tirelessly, day in and day out, that the Establishment fears nothing so much as working-class whites and working-class blacks getting themselves together. Because when that day comes, brother, the system is going to change.
>
> This is the role of the black elected official.

Is this just more rhetoric? Perhaps. But it is rhetoric with a different ring, a different emphasis. If more elected officials— black and white—began to even *talk* this way, they would be setting a new political stage; they would be raising new questions and charting new possible courses for the society. Such courses point the way, on the one hand, to viable, significant change, while, on the other, keep the society from wrenching apart along racial lines. The black elected officials like Richard Hatcher constitute, in a real sense, a kind of last hope for the society. As Dr. Martin Luther King Jr. was in the pressure politics arena, so Mayor Hatcher is in the arena of electoral politics—that is, a major linkage figure. He is attempting to link the black with the white, the young with the old, the traditional with the modern, the *process* of politics with the *fact* of significant change. He has the confidence of street gangs in Gary's ghettos as well as the ear of top national political and economic decision-makers. There are not many people in American public (or private) life today who can legitimately perform such linkage roles.

Whether local Gary or national America has the wisdom to perceive this is still an open question. It is open precisely because electing Hatcher to office is not enough; a few successful reforms are not enough. There must be more. There must be a fundamental transformation in the way America performs its affairs, as well as in the distribution of the results of those affairs.

America's story of greatness—if there is to be one—in the latter third of the twentieth century will turn not on how long she kept her military forces in Southeast Asia, not on how long she supported racist regimes in southern Africa, not on how long she repressed legitimate dissent within her own borders, not on how long she procrastinated in dealing with urgent problems of poverty at home. If America is to have a story of greatness in the latter third of the twentieth century, that story will turn on how long she kept men like Richard G. Hatcher in public office, and on how long she helped their records of success to be.

In the final analysis, it is not Richard Hatcher's administration that is put to the test. Let us be clear that it is America's viability and veracity as a modern society that is being challenged. And if she fails, let us not blame the Dick Hatchers. Rather, the blame will be America's for not supporting the new men of modernity like Mayor Richard Hatcher of Gary, Indiana.

CHARLES V. HAMILTON

Professor of Political Science
Columbia University
New York, New York

June, 1970

Introduction

EVER SINCE its 1966 rebirth, the Black Power ideology has been a loosely-knit collection of ideals celebrating the beauty of the black physique, the glories of ancient black civilizations, and the essential tragedy and triumph of the black experience in America. Afro hairdos, colorful da-ishikis, a blossoming of black arts, an explosion of black studies—these have been among the more obvious aspects of a value transformation still germinating in the black community. This "cultural revolution" has helped blacks generate pride in themselves and their cultural creations. It has en-hanced their power of self-definition and self-assertion. It has not, however, given them a grip on any of six basic levers of economic and political power in the United States.[1]

It has not helped them control (1) large accumulations of private wealth, (2) any of the two hundred largest corpora-tions, (3) any part of the military-industrial complex which overlaps these corporations, (4) the federal and state govern-mental apparatus, (5) the crime syndicate, or (6) organized labor. In short, black people are still powerless in a nation which dotes on power.

To illustrate, ghetto economics are such that black income

1. Robert S. Browne, "Toward An Overall Assessment of Our Alternatives," *The Review of Black Political Economy*, vol. 1, no. 1 (Spring/Summer 1970), p. 18.

is half, and black unemployment nearly three times the national average. In the business world, not one black firm ranks among the five hundred largest U.S. corporations and only two are listed on a major stock exchange. Indeed, the forty-five thousand black-owned businesses are less than 1 percent of the nation's five-million total. Only the forty-six black-owned insurance companies border on business bigness, but all of them lumped together control only 0.2 percent of the industry's total assets. Together, they are smaller than the sixtieth largest white insurance firm. Similarly, the biggest black-owned bank—Harlem's Freedom National, with deposits of $28 million—does not even rank as one of the nation's one thousand largest.

Of course, the historical reasons for this black economic impotence boil down to slavery and segregation. Blacks simply "did not get in when the melon was being cut." Today, they are numerically too small and too dispersed a group to seize control of any of the power levers in economist Robert S. Browne's listing. Thus the degree of self-determination they can achieve while floundering, like Jonah in the belly of a white whale, is extremely limited. What self-determination they do achieve will come about, Browne argues, largely through political maneuvering. He contends:

> Our tactic must be to utilize cleverly what strength we do have, namely the political force of 25 million potentially united black minds, for extracting some economic resources from those who do have them . . . we have an excellent potential for exercising a sort of negative power, a limited veto so to speak over how the white establishment uses its power. And we should work toward building this sort of power, essentially I suppose via the electoral process but not forgetting that our brothers in the streets have been rather creative about devising other techniques as well.[2]

2. Browne, Ibid.

If Browne's thesis is correct—and it seems more persuasive than suicidal notions about armed revolution or wishful notions of a geographically separate black nation in the United States[3]—then the mayoralties of Gary, Indiana, Cleveland, Ohio, and Newark, New Jersey, merit careful scrutiny as working models of organized black political power. At the very least, they provide blacks vitally needed opportunities to gain the political skills and experiences already attained by other ethnic groups in American political history. Anticipating objections to this general strategy, Stone asks: "If black people refuse to operate within the system in the belief they will be co-opted, what kind of alternatives are open to acquire black power and insure black survival?"[4]

Neither armed revolution, geographical separation within U.S. borders nor a return to Mother Africa are practical or probable. Blacks can, however, maximize their political potential. Never before in the nation's history have they had as great a chance to gain political power. While blacks were still shaking off slavery, Irish Catholics were becoming big city bosses of corrupt but efficient political machines. While blacks were being denied the right to vote, Jews were breaking through the power structures of certain states and cities where they had numerical clout. In a few northeastern states and cities, Italians, in recent years, have begun to displace the Irish, as both the political bosses and the political representatives. Poles, too, have made their political presence felt in certain midwestern urban areas. But blacks have played a minor role as protagonists in the nation's political history. From the beginning of their centuries-long trauma as slaves to their ordeal as second-class citizens, they have been taught

3. For a separatist alternative to geographical separation, see Roy Innis, "Separatist Economics: A New Social Contract," *Black Economic Development* (Englewod Cliffs, N.J.: Prentice Hall, Inc., 1969), pp. 50–59.

4. Chuck Stone, "Black Politics," *The Black Scholar*, vol. 1, no. 2 (1969), p. 8.

that power is a commodity reserved for white people. While a few blacks enjoyed voting rights before the Emancipation Proclamation, none were elected to any important office.[5]

During Reconstruction, however, blacks gained such state offices as Supreme Court justice, lieutenant governor, secretary of state, state treasurer, superintendent of public instruction, and virtually every other public office except that of governor. They were well represented in state constitutional conventions, especially in South Carolina, Louisiana, Florida and Virginia, but at no time controlled the affairs of any state.

Blacks enjoyed their new political opportunities only briefly. By 1902 not a single black man served in a state legislature or in the national Congress. To keep blacks from voting, southern whites set up property and poll tax requirements, the famous "grandfather clause" and the "lily-white" primary. It took nearly ninety years, countless lawsuits before the U.S. Supreme Court, four federal civil rights acts and an anti-poll tax amendment to modestly alleviate the voting imbalance created by the return of "home rule" to the former rebel states. Today, however, numerous blacks in the South still are not permitted to register and vote. This is true even though black registration has nearly doubled to 740,000 in the six states covered by the 1965 Voting Rights Act. Only 62 percent of the South's voting-age blacks are registered as compared with 78 percent of voting-age whites. Some two million blacks must still be registered. Furthermore, no black man represents a southern state in Congress.

In the North, black political impotence is not too dissimilar despite heavy concentrations of blacks in urban areas. Only one black serves among the 100 U.S. senators. Only nine—or about 2 percent—of 435 U.S. representatives are black. If it were a purely mathematical matter, blacks, who

5. Chuck Stone, *Black Political Power in America* (New York: Bobbs-Merrill Company, Inc., 1968) , p. 25.

are about 11 percent of the U.S. population, would have at least forty-eight seats in the House.

The scarcity of blacks in Congress reflects the generally minor role they have played in determining public policy, dispensing jobs, administering government, selecting political candidates and, above all, controlling the political process. For the most part, black politicians have been pawns hand-picked by white structures. The typical "Negro leader" has been a loyal but uninspired party regular. Only one or two of the half-dozen or so blacks in the U.S. House during the greater part of the 1960s have pressed any serious campaign for racial legislation on behalf of their constituents. In other words, black politicians have not been truly responsive to the black community. Black visibility has not automatically meant Black Power. A notable exception is Mayor Richard G. Hatcher.

In his 1967 election campaign, he did not romanticize black political power. Rather, he worked diligently to bring it about. This did not mean that individual whites could not help. They helped generously. But Hatcher was elected primarily because blacks responded to the spirit of his campaign plea: "Let's Get Ourselves Together." Indeed, the Gary victory was not so much a tribute to interracial cooperation as it was evidence of the steadily increasing voting strength of blacks in some cities and their growing ability to organize and vote together when racial interests are at stake. Gary was a longtime Democratic stronghold, but white Democrats bolted in droves rather than vote for a black man. Blacks accounted for more than 90 percent of Hatcher's 39,339-vote total.

Gary symbolizes the increasing importance of black political power in major cities. While pressing for community control of schools, hospitals and other institutions in their communities, blacks can also plan realistically to control their cities. Black stewardship of resources controlled by municipal officials could be the key to the development of black economic and political power that speaks to the needs of the black masses.

Blacks are rapidly becoming numerical majorities in the largest and most important cities in the country. Already they make up more than 59 percent of the populations in Washington, D.C., Newark, N.J., and Gary, Indiana. They were more than 30 percent of the populations in seven of the nation's twelve largest cities in 1968. Their numbers practically doubled in Los Angeles and New York between 1950 and 1968. Politically, all of this means that blacks are now in position by virtue of their numbers to influence decisions and the outcome of elections in major municipalities more powerfully than any other ethnic group. They can take over city administrations by electing fellow blacks to major offices in city government. In short, their concentration in major cities has put within their reach the capacity to overcome their historically powerless status and to operate in the political system from a position of strength.

Black control of city hall, then, seems a reasonable first step toward the development of black political power. Such control will be increasingly possible during the 1970s, because of the black in-migration and the white out-migration which characterizes most of the nation's larger cities. If present population trends continue, by 1971 there will be a black majority, or close to it, in Detroit, Baltimore, St. Louis, Compton, California, and Richmond, Virginia. These five cities are quite likely to see blacks running for mayor the next time around—blacks who have a solid chance of winning. Jacksonville, Florida, and New Orleans, Louisiana, also are headed for black majorities by 1971. But there is some doubt whether these and other southern cities will have the black voting strength and the political organization to elect black mayors that soon. Further, if present black population trends continue, by 1977 ten other cities could have black mayors: Philadelphia, Chicago, Cincinnati, Columbus, Youngstown and Dayton, Ohio, Camden and Trenton, New Jersey, Oakland and Berkeley, California.

In short, black mayors in fifteen cities now headed by whites could be a reality before the end of this decade. At first glance it appears that blacks will merely gain control of white-abandoned urban misery. But with the control of city government comes a significant degree of political and economic leverage. The power of appointive office, the taxing power, the power to disburse municipal revenues, etc.—all of this will be in black hands. Blacks will be able to tailor law enforcement and education to black needs, monitor the myriad avenues of municipal corruption, and control recurring invasions of their communities by urban renewal (a euphemism for black removal), highway construction, and public works programs. That's power! They will be able to divert funds, now being spent on less needy citizens, to improve their community services and facilities. That's power! They will be able to fix budget allocations for services and projects, approve construction plans, and decide whether to pass on requests for state and federal grants. And that's power!

Each of these decisions will be occasions for blacks to force concessions from other groups. They can force employers who want city contracts to hire and promote blacks. Similarly, they can force unions to open up to blacks by blocking approvals for new construction or by threatening to reform archaic building codes on which their jobs partly depend. As municipal government officials, blacks can override resistance to public housing in so-called white areas and enforce bans on discrimination in the rental and sale of housing.

Finally, strong local black organizations capable of promoting enlightened electoral participation and consistent political discipline will contribute to greater black influence in national politics. To build such organizations, black leaders will need the public office platform to articulate black interests, and public office resources to reward their followers. For all these reasons, the city is a beachhead for black political power.

But it would be shortsighted for blacks to assume that their control of the city will come about automatically through their increasing numerical superiority. Nor will mere Black Power rhetoric bring it about. Blacks are challenged to organize themselves and work for political power as diligently as they did in Gary. There is no mystique about political organizing, no pat formula, no magic gimmick. It is the gruelling, unglamorous work of doorbell ringing, telephoning, caucusing, speech-making, and fund-raising. It is long hours of labor with little or no immediate prospect of compensation. It is teamwork, a nearly total dedication to a larger cause, a submergence of individual self-interests to those of the group.

While there is no single blueprint for political organizing, Hamilton lists at least three rudimentary processes which can make such activity effective,[6] processes which, incidentally, undergirded the Gary election campaign. The first involves the simple act of counting, that is, determining the number of actual or potential voters in a given precinct, ward or congressional district. The second involves the organizing of a core group or cadre which Hamilton suggests should not be larger than living-room size. This is the brain trust and money trust. Members of this core group may differ on ideology and strategy, but once a consensus is reached it is obligatory for the entire group to support it. In other words, commitment to each other should transcend differences over ideology or strategy. The third phase of political structuring involves the

6. Columbia University political scientist Charles V. Hamilton articulated these principles in a "Political Development" workshop at a February 1968 Chicago convention of the National Unitarian Universalist Black Caucus.

organizing of the masses around bread-and-butter issues and the push for new voter registration. These processes aim ultimately for actual—not symbolic—victories so as to develop a "winner mentality" in the community being organized.

Will such organizing of the black electorate to take over the cities prove futile in the long run? Some students of politics are alarmed at the growing movement to subordinate city governments to the administration of regional metropolitan areas. They see this as a way of thwarting black political empowerment. They suspect, in other words, that just as blacks are nibbling at the edges of political power, others are busily laying plans to snatch it away. Hamilton, however, argues that regional metropolitan government is not necessarily an enemy of the cities. Because of its expanded tax base, it may be a more effective way of dealing with such broad problems as air pollution, water pollution, mass transportation, higher education, advanced medical care, etc.[7]

Indeed, it seems clear that no local administration can completely extricate itself from the American urban quagmire. Only radical changes in the national scene can make the ultimate difference. But Gary's Mayor Richard G. Hatcher, in particular, has shown that local leadership can make a significant beginning. It can begin to initiate a dialogue between the affluent society and "the other America," between white fear and black rage. It can begin to level the black ghetto before it levels itself, begin to replace shack with bungalow, begin to transfer the power to make programmatic decisions from the establishment to those—the nameless ones—whose lives are most directly affected, begin to instill in the disenchanted and long-ignored black, brown and white, a new sense of pride and achievement.

In other words, the thrust of Hatcher's administration has

7. Charles V. Hamilton, "Conflict, Race and System-Transformation in the United States," *Journal of International Affairs*, vol. 23, no. 1 (1969) , p. 116.

been toward "new politics," toward citizen participation in city government. He has nominated millworkers and house-wives as well as prominent citizens to advisory boards and committees in the belief that control of government by the governed is at the heart of the democratic ethic. He is con-vinced that political black power—the organizing and efficient use of the electoral process by the black community—is on the upsurge. His optimism is rooted as much in the relative suc-cess of his own administration as in evidences of black polit-ical empowerment elsewhere in the nation. So it is to his administration that this book turns with the modest aims of describing how Gary's blacks organized themselves to take over city hall, what differences their rise to political power have made to the city and whether any of their political experiences are transferable to other urban areas with large black popula-tions.

But much of this book is also a political profile of Mayor Hatcher, a profile which only suggests some of the connections between his life experiences and his public career and does not pretend to be biographically exhaustive. When the Mayor completed law school in 1959, he, like many others, was fight-ing for "integration." He still is. But he wants it after blacks have developed an economic and political power base from which they can define the terms of racial equality in America.

I am indebted to Mayor Hatcher for the many hours, un-der the pressure of impossible schedules and endless demands, when he made himself available for tape-recorded interviews. I am also grateful for the assistance of such other Gary citizens as Controller Jesse Bell, Executive Secretary Ray Wild, for-mer city officials Arthur Naperstack and Edward Grier, former Corporation Counsel Hilbert Bradley, City Councilmen Doz-ier Allen and Quinton Smith, Urbanologist Joyce Whitley, Dr. James T. Jones, Gary Board of Health Administrator

John Lawshe, Housing Administrator Jack Russell, and Valparaiso University law professor Bertrand Wechsler.

Most of the sketch of Mayor Hatcher's early life comes from his father, Carlton Hatcher, and stepmother Georgia Hatcher; from his sisters, Collie Wise, Gladys Givan and Margie Davis; and his brother, Charles. For editorial assistance with the manuscript I am indebted to Dr. Charles Hamilton of the Columbia University Political Science Department, Dr. Robert McKersie of the University of Chicago Graduate Business School, Illinois State Senator Richard Newhouse, *Ebony* Magazine editor Herbert Nipson, Chicago stock broker Victoria Lynn Sanders and William Strickland, a Senior Fellow at the Institute of the Black World in Atlanta, Ga. Only the author is responsible for errors of fact or interpretation.

ALEX POINSETT

Chicago, 1970

1. The Patch

1. The Patch

I LEFT MACON, Georgia, in September 1921 and came to Michigan City, Indiana. I had a wife and four children then. I didn't think I could ever bring them up in a country like this. It was too cold for my folks. I went back home in March of the next year. But I had to leave in a hurry.

I had worked with this saw mill owner for about fifteen years. I used to work from sun-up to sun-down for two dollars a day. Sometimes when he had a special order, I even had to work all night long loading a freight car. He wanted me to come back to work for him, because he knew he could depend on me. I finally told him if I stayed in Macon, I would work for him again. But he couldn't wait. He just went right down and got a warrant. He was going to have me arrested to make me stay in Georgia. He knowed if he got me in jail, I would give in. You know how they do down there. They just tell the sheriff to arrest that Negro and that's it.

The sheriff was going down Poplar Street looking for me that same evening. I had my wife's uncle's car getting some groceries to take out to him. I seed the sheriff, but I didn't pay him no attention. I guess he didn't see me. I got out to my wife's uncle's place

and my wife's mother told me don't come in because
the sheriff was looking for me. I told her to tell my
wife to bring my overcoat. I had my money in my
pocket. A friend drove me back to Macon that night,
but I was afraid to catch a train there. I was afraid
the sheriff would be at the terminal looking for me.
So I went up to Vinesville. That's right up from
Macon. I got a train there. By the help of the Lord,
I got out from there.

The short, white-haired man reminiscing in the dining room of his neat Michigan City bungalow is the father of Richard (Dick) Hatcher, mayor of Gary, Indiana. A generation of history separates the father's *running from* Macon, Georgia, and the son's *running of* Gary, Indiana. Yet much of the father is recapitulated in the son. Much of his religiosity, his tenacity, his shrewdness, his sense of fair play are reflected in the son's life style.

Unusually short but still robust from a lifetime of hard work, Carlton Hatcher is between seventy-five and eighty years old. He doesn't know for sure, because when he was born most black people were not issued birth certificates. But even if he had one, he still would be unable to read it, because where he grew up in Georgia most black kids were allowed only one or two years of schooling—if any. And even if they attended school, it was for only three or four months a year. There was cotton to be picked on the sprawling farms of white folks, or corn to be harvested, or trees to be felled. By the time Carlton Hatcher was maybe eleven—he doesn't know for sure—he was already doing the work of "most any man." Gangs of black kids worked at the saw mill from sun-up to sun-down for sixty cents a day.

Carlton Hatcher was savoring all those wonderful stories he had heard about the promised land up North when he brought his wife and four children to Michigan City in 1921, some twelve years before Dick's birth (July 10, 1933). He had come believing he could make life a little easier for his family. But the good life is relative. Maybe he wouldn't be harassed by a Georgia sheriff, but he had to contend with ruthless landlords and creditors. Maybe his pay was now six dollars instead of two dollars a day, but his job of molding railroad car wheels at the Pullman Standard Works in Michigan City still stretched him out rubber-like from dawn to dusk. Maybe he no longer had to live in a rural Georgia shack, but a wind-buffeted frame house in "the Patch" in mid-Winter was in many ways even worse.

No one quite knows why that little black settlement in Michigan City was called "the Patch" back in the days before it was "urban renewed" into a low-income housing development. Maybe its small size suggested the label. Maybe it was a blot on the rest of the world, a self-contained smudge of blacks who were resigned to an isolation imposed from outside. Maybe it was the archetypal ghetto where a sensitive kid like Dick Hatcher could feel and suffer and resolve to grow up someday and change it all.

The Patch was only a block-long street running into Lake Michigan. Wooden shacks lined both sides of what amounted to an unpaved alley. Once they were single-family dwellings. Now they were homes for two, three, sometimes four families. The Hatchers shared one of those houses—a weather-beaten, two-story, six-room frame—with Collie Belle, the family's second-oldest child, and her husband. In fact, very early in his boyhood Dick Hatcher's secret ambition was to grow up and own an ice box he could raid at will. The Hatcher's ice box was shared by two families and sometimes he was whipped for accidentally snacking on food that did not belong to his family.

A bow-legged, fat-bellied, cast iron coal stove dominated

the living room downstairs. Sometimes the only way the
Hatcher kids could get coal for it was by stealing from coal
cars on the railroad tracks across the street. Dick says: "I still
remember how unhappy we would be when my father would
tell us that we had to let the fire go down at night because
otherwise there woudn't be enough coal the next day." And
even when there was enough coal, the heat was so uneven that
two of the Hatcher infants—a set of twins—died of pneumonia
contracted while crawling around on the drafty floors. Nevertheless, Katherine Hatcher mothered thirteen children and
although the physical stress was sometimes trying, having children, as her oldest daughter, Gladys, explains, "was just something that she felt she was supposed to do." Gladys cannot recall ever seeing her mother having fun. "I guess it wasn't
anything that she missed," the daughter says. "She seemed con-
tented." Katherine Hatcher was content to accept her husband's dominant role in their home and although she may
have disagreed with him on occasion, she never really allowed
herself to argue with him before her children. Indeed, so far
as they knew, not a harsh word ever passed between their
parents.

Such tranquility was quite unusual in the Patch, where life
was usually more turbulent. Some escaped it momentarily in
a makeshift hotel down near the corner of the block, buying
bootleg whiskey and shooting dice, playing blackjack or
patronizing one of the resident prostitutes. Those who aspired
for a better life, as did the Hatchers, dreamed of owning a
home across town in East Port where Carlton Hatcher lives
today.

The Depression did not hit white America until 1929, but
it had been a way of life for blacks long before. Mere survival
was a victory of sorts in the Patch. Most families received
public aid, or what in those days was called "commodities"—
powdered milk, powdered eggs, dried prunes, sacks of potatoes

and fruit, and cellophane packages of glossy white margarine
ready to be kneaded with little pellets of yellow dye. "We
were on relief and I didn't know we were on relief," recalls
Dick Hatcher. "I thought that was the way life was."

In dietary terms, life in the Patch was the fine art of sur-
viving on neckbones, brains, blackeyed peas and cornbread
long before "soul food" became gourmet cuisine. Small for his
age in those boyhood years, Dick nevertheless was such a big
eater that his father often suggested, teasingly, that the extra
weight made him "too po' (too small) to tote it." Back in
Georgia, a man could just about feed his family adequately
from his own little truck garden. Maybe Carlton Hatcher
couldn't buy them the best clothes and house them in a man-
sion, but he could feed them well on greens and beans and
whatever else a garden grows. Up North, on the other hand,
a man could earn more money than he had "down home" and
still his family might not have enough to eat. So the Hatchers
improvised. Often they took buckets and pans and joined
their neighbors down at the waterfront to welcome incoming
fishing boats and receive gifts of fish too small for marketing.

Sundays around the Hatcher household were holy days de-
voted almost exclusively to hours of worship in a Baptist
church where Carlton Hatcher served as a deacon. But one of
those Sundays marked an event which almost certainly altered
the direction of Dick's life while he was still only nursery-
school age. Instead of going to church that evening with his
mother, father, and youngest sister, Margie, he remained
home to pal around with a playmate up the street. Along
about dusk, when objects begin to lose their shape and color
and the world seems to descend into itself, Dick and his friend
were "chunkin'" rocks at each other. It was not so much a
rock fight as it was an enactment once again of that age-old
boyhood ritual, the perpetual testing of throwing skill. Little
boys are nearly always too adventuresome and daring to

worry about the potential danger to life and limb of a thrown
rock. Besides, they throw not so much to hit their competitors
as to barely miss them and thus, as a baseball pitcher would
say of menacing batters, "keep them honest." Dick and his
friend were testing each other when it happened: a rock
slammed into Dick's left eye. The fateful night trembled with
his screams. Tenderly, his mother bathed the wounded eye
with salt water and tucked him in bed. But the pain would not
let him sleep. He "just hollered all night long," brother
Charles remembers.

Carlton Hatcher had not understood that his son's injury
demanded immediate medical attention. He simply went on
to work the next morning. Returning home that evening, he
found his youngest son still in intense pain. The memory of
it haunts Carlton Hatcher still:

> *I carried him to the doctor. He treated him for
> three or four days, but it didn't get any better. I
> carried him to another specialist. He should have
> taken it out, because the ball was busted. But Mama
> thought maybe he could see out of it again. It went
> on about a year, then it began to bother the other
> eye. Then I had to have it taken out. I spent about
> six or seven hundred dollars. I wasn't working none
> hardly. When I carried him to this specialist, he ad-
> mitted him in the hospital but he wouldn't touch
> him until I brought him seventy-five dollars that
> next day; and brother, seventy-five dollars was some-
> thing in those days. But you know, when the Lord
> is for you, who can be against you? I was working
> just one or two days a week. I went to my company
> office and before I could tell my foreman what I
> wanted, he told me I could get it. He gave me
> the seventy-five dollars and I carried it on to*

*the hospital. That evening they went to work on
Richard.*

The operation, Dick's glass eye replacement, his new glasses
—all strained an already meager family budget. Like most
black families, then and now, the Hatchers were forced to
have two bread-winners. Dick's mother worked a half block
around the corner of the Patch in a factory that polluted the
air for miles with the stench of rotting pig tails. In this slaugh-
terhouse setting Mrs. Hatcher and her fellow workers—all
black women—flanked both sides of a conveyor belt covered
with the tails and swarms of flies. Meticulously they stripped
the tails of hair that was used later to stuff furniture cushions.
For every pound they picked, they received a stupendous
three cents.

Aside from the pungent odor, Dick Hatcher still remembers
running home from school almost daily to earn a few pennies
as an errand boy for the women at the hair factory. On Saturdays, he and his cronies were even more enterprising, scour-
ing the alleys on "junking" expeditions, collecting paper, bot-
tles, cardboard boxes and selling them to a junk yard that
bordered the Patch. "That is what my father also did for a
living during the Depression when he could only work two
or three days a week at Pullman Standard," the son recalls.
"He used to bring all this junk home and we'd jump up and
down on it to pack it down for him. After I got to be about
eleven or twelve, we used to go out ourselves. It was ridiculous what we got—maybe twenty-five cents for a whole day's
junk."

But junking was an apprenticeship which for some of
Dick's young friends, eventually became a lifetime of "hus-
tling." Some were better hustlers than others. "We used to go
downtown with big overcoats," Dick recalls, "and steal from
the dime stores. It wasn't right, but it was hard to be honest

when you didn't have anything and were very young and so very poor."

For black kids like Dick during the Depression, the struggle for survival was more pressing than the need for education. "I remember many days when I didn't go to school because I didn't have shoes," he recalls. "More often, when I did go, I remember how embarrassed I was because the shoes had holes in them. With three older brothers, I was always wearing hand-me-downs, and I recall the great thrill and delight I felt when I got the first suit I ever owned. I must have been sixteen years old."

During their two-month summer vacations away from school, Dick and his friends worked at the resort homes of wealthy Jews at nearby Long Beach, cutting grass, trimming hedges, scrubbing floors, or shoveling sand that constantly sifted in on the properties.

"Sometimes I'd work all day in somebody's yard shoveling that sand," Dick remembers. "After you got through, they would look at the job and if they didn't like it, they would say, 'I'm not going to pay you.' There was nothing you could do about it. You couldn't go to the police or anything like that."

But if the work crew—usually four or five boys—satisfied the employer, they received two dollars to divide among themselves. Often as the children of these wealthy Jews played on the swings and slides at a nearby amusement park, coins, nearly always stuffed in their pockets, would fall unnoticed to the ground. So some days, instead of going to Long Beach to work, young Hatcher and his cronies would root around the play equipment for lost treasures.

Money was always scarce around the Hatcher household, but no matter, the Hatchers were rich in religious faith, a fundamentalist kind of faith that said an all-seeing, ever-present, infinitely-powerful, heavenly Father would always provide for those who were humble and obedient. It was a kind of fundamentalism that pictured God as a cosmic expression of love for humanity, sacrificing His only son to redeem the sins of the world. The coming of that son into the world, splitting human history, the A.D. from the B.C., was the central focus of Christmas, according to the Hatchers' faith. So if Christmas rolled around and there was no money for gift giving, "well, thank you Jesus" for life and health and food and clothing and shelter.

Somehow, though, Carlton Hatcher and his wife nearly always managed to have enough money to shop downtown on Christmas Eve. To their children left at home, it seemed they would never return. Every few minutes they would go scampering into the street searching for their parents who would finally return loaded down—not with packages of toys but always with practical things like shoes and clothes. The children would take the dollar each was given for Christmas shopping and scurry off to the stores. They had come to understand very early in their young lives that there was no Santa Claus.

Poverty, in fact, meant there was not even a radio in the Hatcher household during a large part of Dick's boyhood. Always, though, there was some one neighbor in the Patch who would let kids, and grownups too, come to hear broadcasts of Joe Louis's fights. And there were always spontaneous festivals whenever the champ won. Young and old folks danced in the streets, because Joe was one of the few black men anywhere in the universe, for all they knew, who was really "making it" in the hostile white world. Rejoicing in his boxing prowess was a socially safe way for blacks to siphon off some of the venom brewed by oppressive white racism.

When Dick's family could finally afford a radio, Joe Louis joined other heroes. There was "The Lone Ranger" galloping off on his swift, white horse, "Silver," and the "G-r-r-r-e-e-n

Hornet" and that basso profoundo, "The Sha-a-dow" with his sinister bursts of laughter and the scary, creaking door of "Inner Sanctum". Yesterday's radio was more real than to-day's television could ever be. Even so, the coming of TV to the Hatcher household was a momentous event in Dick's boyhood:

My sister and brother-in-law finally bought a house and they moved out. By that time they had had two kids. As soon as they moved out another couple moved in. They were an elderly couple, a semi-invalid woman and her husband who every-body called Mr. Ben. He worked for the people who owned the junk yard in Michigan City. They were wealthy people who seemed to accumulate money by the bushel. Mr. Ben was the butler and chauffeur for them and his wife was the maid. In those days that was real prestige—just working for rich white folks.

Anyway, Mr. Ben and his wife lived in one room in our house and they had a TV set. It was one of the first TVs to come out with the screen about 10 by 10 inches. The pictures were terrible. The one thing they enjoyed watching were the wrestling matches. That was the thing! People from all over the neigh-borhood would come down to our house to watch Mr. Ben's TV set. There was a real protocol. When they were gone during the day, we didn't turn the TV set on. Nobody touched it. But man! We couldn't wait for them to get home in the evenings. Of course, his wife had to fix dinner for him and they used our dining room to eat. The dining room was used in shifts. We would eat and then they would eat. We had to wait until she had fixed din-

*ner for him and he sat down and ate. Then he would
say, "Well, I guess I'll go and look at television." Oh
man! He was beautiful! He would sit in the big easy
chair and all of us would get down on the floor. All
my friends would come over and I had a lot of
friends because we had a TV set. He would watch
wrestling until one o'clock at night. Talk about getting involved! The adults too. It was just a regular
thing.*

For young Hatcher and his friends, television was a convenient substitute for the twelve-cent movies on Saturdays
they could not afford to attend unless they had scratched and
scraped their pennies together during the week. But when
you got right down to it, athletics—not television or movies
—were the really "big thing" in the Patch, as Dick remembers. A kid could come to the Elite Youth Center for basketball and ping pong. Sometimes, though, he first had to fist
fight rivals from across town. Youth gangs did not fight with
bicycle chains and knives and guns in those days.

Dick was a baseball player like his three older brothers and
his brother-in-law, all of whom might have made the major
leagues had there been no color bars. As it was, they could
not even play American Legion ball like the white boys in
Michigan City. They were restricted to the sandlots. Richard
was a slightly-wild, fastballing pitcher who preferred playing
shortstop. His team, the Bears, were the Patch's heroes, especially when they beat a lily-white team. It was as if each had
momentarily become a Joe Louis and licked white racism
through sheer athletic ability.

But white racism never really stayed licked. It was always
there in one form or another. Blacks were barred from
Michigan City's YMCA. In fact, the only way they ever
got inside—and then only briefly—was through a city-wide,

junior high school program for beginning swimmers. Dick
remembers:

> *They would first pick the kids in the school and*
> *send them down there. Everybody would line up*
> *along the pool and they would say, "Alright, every-*
> *body dive in and see if you can get across the pool."*
> *They said that was their way of telling who could*
> *swim. They said they didn't want kids getting out of*
> *two hours of classwork by pretending they were*
> *learning how to swim. Somehow it always worked*
> *out that they said to black kids, "You can swim." I*
> *remember when I went there, they ordered me to*
> *dive and I—who can't swim even today—floated*
> *across the pool. And this guy said, "You can swim.*
> *Back to school." That's how they systematically got*
> *rid of all the black kids in the program. I remember*
> *a lot of things like that. Things happened that at*
> *the time I didn't understand. Now, in retrospect, I*
> *understand.*

Much of that insight had come from his father who, while
illiterate, had an abundance of that indefinable homespun
genius some folks call "mother wit". Carlton Hatcher had
developed an almost over-protective attitude toward Dick after
he suffered his eye accident. The bonds between father and
youngest son drew even tighter after the momentous event
of June 1, 1947. Dick was only fourteen at the time. He and
his youngest sister, Margie, were the only two of the seven
living Hatcher children still at home. Their mother had been
ailing for two years. Sometimes Dick would ask her how she
felt and nearly always she would reply, "I feel pretty good,"
or words like that. Sometimes he wanted to know why she had
to sit on the couch or lie on the bed for so long and she would

explain: "Well, my legs hurt." But the inquisitive son began to understand that the mysterious ailment that plagued his mother was far more serious than she would admit, because one day he entered his parents' bedroom and—for the first time in his young life—found his father crying.

As a "sanctified" Baptist, Katherine Hatcher had refused either a doctor or medications. Her fellow church members would come in and pray with her, offering up incantations of their profound faith that God would heal her. But as June 1 approached, Katherine Hatcher, who had melted from buxomness to nearly a skeleton, became progressively less lucid and her husband insisted on bringing in a doctor. He was departing from his fundamentalism in making this concession to the secular, but his religious faith told him his wife was going to live. And one of Katherine's sisters believed that, too. She had come to the house and baked a cake, because June 1 was going to be Margie's twelfth birthday. Her birthday came, but not her party.

Very early that morning, while Margie and Richard were still asleep, Katherine Hatcher began gasping for breath. A half hour later she was dead, a victim of breast cancer at fifty-three. Dick did not cry two days later at the funeral. Somehow, tears seemed inappropriate to him. A feeling of sorrow welled up in him, but the powerful emotion was smothered by his understanding that his mother had suffered greatly and now was not going to suffer any longer. In fact, she was going to her reward in some blissful place that everybody called "heaven." So as Dick contemplated his mother's body lying in state, he was surprised and pleased that she looked no different in death than she had in life.

Yet the death of Katherine Hatcher had made a profound difference for Carlton Hatcher. After thirty-five years of marriage he was a widower with two children to rear. And Margie was at just the age—the onset of puberty—when she needed a mother desperately. He was a church deacon who, on the one hand, had to live a clean, Christian life because "folks watch you", but on the other hand, he needed a wife. Carlton Hatcher was quick, and decisive. Three months after his wife's death, he proposed marriage to a fellow church member. Two months later they were married.

2. The Winding Road Out

2. The Winding Road Out

LONG BEFORE her untimely death, Katherine Hatcher had hoped and prayed fervently that her youngest son would receive a college education. Though uneducated herself, she believed a college degree could be Dick's passport out of the Patch. Because of his eye disability, she had not wanted him to work in a factory as had her husband and their other three sons. And Dick, too, had long aspired for the prestige of a white-collar job. During his pre-grade school days his oldest sister, Gladys, had been a secretary for the only black lawyer in Michigan City. Occasionally she let Dick visit her at the law office and sometimes, he was privileged—as he saw it, from his boyish point of view—to run errands for the lawyer. Oh how Dick admired the lawyer's fine house, his big car, and the air of importance that floated about him. No question about it, the lawyer was his idol. He, too, was going to be a lawyer—no matter what.

Except that Dick's parents had already picked the medical profession for him. After all, doctors, even black doctors, earned a handsome living and were highly respected by everyone. Indeed the only doctor in Michigan City, the doctor who had brought Dick into the world, was so well respected why, by golly, he even "got to talk to white people and they listened to him, too." He was something, all right enough. Why whenever he made a house call everyone acted as if they were

in the presence of the Deity. On one of those visits the doctor
suggested quite authoritatively to Carlton Hatcher that Dick
should—by all means—become a doctor. That was the end of
it. The issue was settled. There would be no more discussion
about whether the boy should choose between doctoring or
lawyering.

But it was not really that simple, since much of Dick's future was left neither to himself nor his parents. Much of it
was in the hands of the white authorities at "integrated"
Elston High School where a principal once expelled Dick for
"talking back" to an art teacher. He had not been sassy by
nature, but how much can a guy take? She would keep Dick
after school, knowing of course that he would miss his usual
evening practice with the school's football team. Or she was
forever praising his artistic ability on the one hand and rap-
ping his knuckles on the other. Like the time he sketched a
woman and a man simply in the act of looking at each
other. Seeing the drawing, the teacher stormed to the other
side of the room and said, as if to no one in particular: "I
don't know what we're going to do about *these people* who
keep drawing these men and women in the final clinches."

Well, one word provoked another and the next thing Dick
knew he was expelled, a major event, because it meant his father had to lose time from his job—and therefore money—to
get him re-admitted. As they sat in the school office, the principal lectured: "Dick, that woman has got what you're trying
to get. You have to get along with her."

Indeed "getting along," accommodating, not challenging
white authority in any way, was the behavior expected of
black students at Elston High. It was their apprenticeship for
the adult life just around the corner. Elston's counselors advised black girls to concentrate on home economics. Why not?
The counselors were simply projecting from past experience
which told them the girls were probably going to end up

working in someone's kitchen, anyway. Lo and behold, their prophecies were nearly always fulfilled.

Elston's counselors steered black boys into vocational courses. "Be realistic!" they pleaded. "You know what's going to happen. You aren't going to college. So you might as well prepare for work at Pullman-Standard." Dick vigorously objected to that sort of counseling in his junior year, when students usually sought advice about their future careers.

"My father doesn't want me to take the vocation course," he explained to the counselor.

"Well, you better go home and talk to your father about it again," she snapped.

But Carlton Hatcher still knew what was best for his son and so the counselor reluctantly permitted Dick to pursue a "commercial course," mainly bookkeeping, typing, business English, and business machine operation. He received little of the academics that would have prepared him for college. That was out of the question. After all, only two black kids in the school's history had gone to college and their very rarity made them celebrities. A doctor's son, for example, had flunked out of three or four colleges. No matter. He was still a celebrity in the black community. He had at least attended college even if only erratically.

Not everyone was so fortunate. Dick's oldest sister, Gladys, had yearned for college when she graduated from Elston High years earlier, but the Depression had eliminated that possibility. A little later, a football scholarship had been brother William's entré to Kentucky State in the early 1940s. But by and large, college was not programmed into the future of the Hatchers and other black youngsters. In fact, considering the rampant racism at Elston High, considering the constant harassment and humiliation of black students by both white teachers and students, black youngsters were lucky even to graduate.

In other words, their graduation was the end of a long and psychologically tortuous obstacle course. Elston High's graduation proms were carefully arranged so that no black student either escorted or was escorted by a white student. In fact, to guarantee strict observance of this racial policy, the school rule which said only seniors could attend graduation proms was conveniently ignored in Dick's junior year. The reason was quite simple: there was one extra black girl in the graduating class, one more, that is, than the number of black boys. She needed an escort. So school officials hastily summoned Dick into their worried presence to explain:

"We would like for you to go to the prom this year."

"Well, juniors can't go to the prom," he replied, innocently.

"That's okay!"

"But, I don't have any money to get a tuxedo or anything like that.

"That's okay!"

School officials were going to rent a tuxedo or anything else Dick needed. All he had to do was cooperate. Disgust welled up in him, instead. He saw himself the pawn in their racial game. He was too proud for that, too proud to be an accommodating, obsequious, little black Sambo. Yet, if he stuck by his pride, then one black girl would have to miss her first and only high school prom. She would be hurt, but she would understand. At least, Dick hoped so. He turned down the school officials cold.

When his own graduation came in June 1952, Dick once again saw the white paranoia that by now had become quite familiar. Normally, students in the academic procession were matched by heights. Such an arrangement on this night would have paired Dick with a white girl. What to do? No problem! School officials simply eliminated pairings by height.

After the graduation ceremonies, Dick bravely announced to his parents that he was determined to enter college even though at that moment, he had no money and little prospect of getting some through a scholarship. He remembers:

The business of scholarships was one of the most traumatic experiences that I had when I was in high school. There were black kids who had the brain power to receive scholarships. But we knew that the scholarships that were being handed out—no matter what kind of grade average you had—were not going to black kids. Those were white scholarships! It was understood. The only scholarships that blacks got were like if some local black church put up maybe like $100. I got two of those. But the white kids were getting like $4,000 to finance their whole college education. It was just a traumatic thing. I feel so sorry for black kids today, because in many cases they are still getting even worse treatment than that. Imagine the scars that are created by that kind of thing. When I was in high school, I stuttered. I had a very bad case of stuttering and I'm sure that was just because of all the frustrations I felt before graduating from Elston High. It was not uncommon. The kids I played with—they stuttered! I'm sure things like that just had to have a psychosomatic base.

No money, no scholarship, no desire to forsake college—that was Dick Hatcher in June, 1952. His parents proposed he enroll at Chicago's Roosevelt University, pointing out he could save money by living with an aunt in Chicago. And since it was less than seventy miles from Michigan City, he could come home on an occasional weekend. But no, Dick was anxious to attend a "real" college, that is, one where he could live on a campus just like his brother William, at Kentucky State.

The school would have to be Indiana University, of course, since it had come through and awarded Dick an athletic stipend to cover his books and tuition. Still, he needed money for room, board, and incidentals. During the 1952 summer he worked first as a dishwasher, later as a laborer loading lumber into freight cars at Pullman-Standard, his father's employer. But the money he earned, plus the two hundred dollars in scholarships awarded to him by the two black churches, was still not enough for college. So sisters Collie Belle and Gladys—"man, they were beautiful"—started taking money out of their grocery allowances for his expenses. And when all that nickel and diming was added up, why the next thing Dick knew he was floating bird-like on a big, sprawling, gently-rolling, tree-studded campus. His dormitory was not like the weather-beaten old army barracks he had seen at Kentucky State. To a bird on a "trip", it was a palace. Dick was a member of royalty, even though, when he returned to the real world, he was reduced to cleaning tables part-time in the dining hall.

If getting into college had been a mountaintop experience for Dick, staying there required all of his skill to keep from tumbling down the slopes. First of all there was the urgent matter of his academic unreadiness. Because of the unofficial tracking system which worked to the disadvantage of black students at Elston High, he had not been taught higher mathematics and was obliged to learn its rudiments at a high school on the Indiana campus. He had not been taught English grammar so that his struggle with the required English composition course at Indiana was "like eating nails." He was shy of the chemistry and other physical sciences he needed so badly for the medical career his parents had picked for him. Before long he convinced them that he should be preparing for anything other than a medical career. He had not been taught a foreign language, a fact that would bedevil his two years of French at Indiana. All around him, black students similarly plagued with poor high school preparation were "flunking out like flies."

"If you saw a good looking girl," Dick laughs now, "you had better talk to her this semester, because she wouldn't be there next semester. That was just understood. I knew it wasn't because of some inherent mental incapacity or anything like that. It was just that we had not gotten it in high school. We were not prepared for college."

In fact, Dick was obliged to quit the football team after his freshman year to concentrate on his studies. Though he knew the typical college athlete had a reputation for not being scholastically inclined, he also knew that they were not so much brainless as lacking in study time because of their participation in athletics. And even when there was time, daily team practice sapped their energy. Dick saw football looming between himself and a successful college career. While he gave up football, he continued on the track team as a high jumper and 220-yard sprinter because he still needed the money from his athletic stipend.

By his sophomore year, Dick's college life as a government major and economics minor had settled into an interminable routine of book reading, lecture listening and term paper writing. Like most of his fellow black students, he did not feel a part of the organic whole that was Indiana University. It was as if there was one campus for him and another for the white students. From the simple matter of where he could get a haircut to the more complex determination of what parties on campus he could attend, college life was a strictly segregated affair. It was not as if anyone ever told him he could not attend campus dances. And there were no "for white only" signs posted on the bulletin boards. It was just that no one ever encouraged or expected him to be quite so bold.

Even campus restaurants like "Nicks" were off limits to Dick and his fellow black students. They could buy food there, all right, but they could not sit and eat on the spot. As if they were something less than civilized human beings, they had to take it elsewhere. What to do about such galling humiliation? It was the sort of challenge that in February 1960 would inspire four students at North Carolina A & T College to stage a lunch counter sit-in at Greensboro and thus spark a student revolt that is still unfolding. In the freezing winter of 1953, Dick and other members of a campus NAACP chapter, counseled by one of his government professors who thought Kenya's Mau Mau brigades should be aided by the U.S. government, staged the nearest thing to a sit-in. They picketed Nicks in shifts. If, for example, Dick had classes from 8 to 12, he would picket from 12:30 to 4. At first the campus restaurant was a Mount Everest of indifference. When it started closing its doors at two in the afternoon, it was a hill with its head no longer in the clouds. Then when its cash receipts started dipping, it flat-out surrendered and started serving black students on the premises.

It was a small but satisfying dent in the racism that mortared the bricks of Indiana University. Still it was not enough to quench the fires of anger and bitterness that were raging in Dick in the wake of his long string of experiences with stupid white people. In his junior year he confided to a family member that he felt he was wasting four years of his life, that he was a man running on a treadmill. He was anxious to get those four college years out of his system and become involved in something that would really be significant. A mayorship maybe? It had not even crossed his mind.

Anxiety and confusion about his future made Dick emotionally vulnerable and he escaped into a brief romantic involvement with a campus white girl. Some of his professors knew about it. They would not be so unscholarly as to make it the subject of their next lecture. Nor would they be so ungentlemanly as to assign supplemental readings on the "problem". The situation called for tact and fatherliness. They would take Dick to one side, maybe tarry with him after class to "reason" with him. There is nothing wrong with interracial dating, they would say. There is nothing wrong with you, Dick, dating a white girl. But take the advice of one who is older and more experienced—persons who involve themselves in interracial dating are asking for trouble. Besides, Dick, people must understand their role in life.

He learned the lesson well and in fact could have earned an "A" if he had been quizzed. It was quite simple: little, nappy-headed black boys were not to mess with white girls at Indiana University. Well, he was a senior now and in a matter of months the school would be behind him. So why spoil everything, because of a friendly white girl? Dick had the patience. Unfortunately, he did not have the good luck he needed.

Before returning to the campus after the Thanksgiving break of his senior year, Dick had stuffed in his pocket a handful of firecrackers his father brought back from a Georgia vacation. The firecrackers lay untouched on the desk in his dormitory room until about two weeks before the end of the semester.

For most of the students at Indiana University, like college students everywhere, the approaching semester break was a restless time, a time of last-minute cramming for finals, a time of bull sessions to break the grind, and a time of horseplaying to ease the tension. During one of those tension-releasing, horseplaying, bull sessions in Dick's room, someone wondered mischievously: what would happen if a firecracker exploded in the hall? Nothing to do but find out. They tried one. Wham! Then another. Wham! Then another, each time lighting the fuse then scurrying back into Dick's room and slamming the door. The sounds in the echo chamber-like hall were not those of exploding firecrackers. They were bombs.

By now nearly everyone was awake and the dormitory trembled with angry curses. Through the hall door burst the headmaster, his face a red scowl, wanting to know who was responsible for the disturbance. Nobody, of course. "I don't know who is to blame," he grunted in response to the deafening silence, "but I think it's Joe and so if nobody has anything to say then he's the one."

Dick fell for the headmaster's feint. He knew, of course, that Joe was not guilty—the actual offenders had escaped. But an unwritten code, binding among men confronting a common enemy, told him he was not to betray his friends. Still, he could not let an innocent man be punished. So he settled the matter to his own satisfaction: he lied that he was the culprit. There was nothing noble about him taking the rap, he thought. There would be no serious consequences. At the very worse, he would be severely scolded and then turned loose, he believed.

The headmaster ordered Dick to report to the official in charge of the entire dormitory complex. It was well past midnight when he confronted the official who was obviously peeved because of his interrupted sleep. Thumbing through a book with a long passage underlined in red, he urged Dick to read. The underlined passage was a section of the Indiana Code explaining that anyone in possession of pyrotechnics was guilty of a misdemeanor. Then Dick read a similar section from the University's book of regulations. It too commented gravely on the offense. Such an offender, it continued ominously, *shall be discharged immediately from the university.*

"You have to be kidding," he said incredulously. "You're not going to do that."

"There's nothing I can do about it," the official replied. "That's the rule and there are no exceptions."

The explanation was paralyzing in its directness. In his stupor it did not occur to Dick that he could still explain he was not guilty and thus avoid expulsion. Instead, he wanted to know: "When will I have to go home?"

"Tomorrow morning!"

"Two weeks before finals? I lose a whole semester?"

"I'm sorry, but nothing can be done about it. You might as well go and start packing."

Dick left the room angrily. The next morning he learned from the Dean of Students that he would have to leave university housing immediately but would be permitted to remain enrolled as a student long enough to complete his final examinations. Although he was a non-fraternity man, he moved that same day into the Kappa Alpha Psi house. The last two weeks before his finals were an eternity.

Dick's body was about to leave Bloomington, but his mind would not adjust to the grim reality that he was no longer a college student. Because of a trivial prank he had not even committed, all of his grand hopes and dreams had been shattered. He had failed his family and friends back home in Michigan City. He had failed his deceased mother. Above all, he had failed himself. Life had suddenly become meaningless, absurd, empty. Dick phoned his father to report: "Papa, I'm leaving school. I'm going to get a job in New York." He did not explain the real reason he was leaving the University and it was several days before his father learned.

Carlton Hatcher was anxious to reach his son again, but Dick had already left the campus. Where was he? Was he well? Was he alive? The anxious questions reduced Dick's father to tears. He believed his son was making a mistake.

In the hope that Dick might find his way to Louisville,

Kentucky, stopping off for at least a little while at his uncle's house. Carlton Hatcher desperately phoned his oldest brother, pleading: "For God's sake, let me know as soon as Richard arrives."

But Dick did not want to face his family. It took his uncle about three weeks to persuade him he should talk with his parents and when he finally phoned, his father begged him to return home. "We understand," he said. But the disconsolate son could not be persuaded. He went to an aunt in Chicago instead.

There in that five-mile stretch of public housing projects surrounding the Dearborn homes at 31st and State, there among those twenty-eight thousand black folk stacked like so much hay in so many high rise barns, there at last Dick could lose himself, at least for a time. And he would get a job. The newspaper ads were full of jobs. Let's see. Take your pick. Bookkeeper maybe? Now carefully fill out the application and don't forget to mention three and a half years of college. Then hear the white man say: "I'm sorry, we need someone with a degree." Or listen to the white lady: "You have too much education for this. You would not want this. It doesn't pay enough. But if anything else opens up, we'll call you."

Don't give up. Every morning, get up and run downtown. Try the Continental Bank. Didn't they advertise for management trainees and executive trainees? No college was required, they said. So how about a job, mister? Thanks for nothing.

Keep trying. Keep getting up and getting knocked down. Keep coming back home and phoning the companies and finding the jobs are still open. Try introducing yourself to another white man on the phone. Hear him say: "Come right down. You're just the man we're looking for." Then show up. Like the company just went out of business.

Niggers—long niggers, short niggers, black niggers, light niggers, ugly niggers, handsome niggers, educated niggers, ignorant niggers—niggers are for washing dishes. So wash the dishes, nigger. Your "edjamakashun" was for washing dishes.

The rebuffs, the rebukes, the repudiations, the unfairness of it, the utter stupidity of it, the hopelessness—it was mind-blowing. It was an invitation for Dick to sink into the water closet of himself and flush into oblivion. He thrashed about for a lifeline. Somewhere in the harbored part of him that was still sane blinked the thought that he could still make it. After all, he was too close to a college degree not to actually receive one. And once that was in hand, he could prepare himself for a livelihood that would not depend on the whim and caprice of white people. After one semester and one summer of suspension from Indiana University, he applied for readmission then returned that September determined never again to relive his ordeal. Standing under a shade tree on graduation day, he told his father: "Papa, I made a big mistake. I'm going through now—all the way! I'm going to be a lawyer. I won't make that mistake again."

Dick's academic work at Indiana University had landed him on the dean's list during the two years before his suspension. But he had been especially studious—a straight-A student—after his readmission, because he feared school officials might find another excuse to dismiss him. His academic record helped persuade three law schools, Indiana, Notre Dame and Valparaiso, that they should admit him. He choose "Valpo" mainly because he had once worked at the nearby Norman Beatty Memorial Hospital and his working there again would help pay his law school expenses. His starting salary would be $205 a month and climb to $245 by the time of his law school graduation three years later. For only $40 a month he would be receiving room, board, and maid service on the hospital grounds. The remainder of his income would not only take care of his law schooling but also enable him to keep up the monthly payments on a Ford on which his father would make a down payment.

Dick attended Valpo from eight to four in the afternoon. By five he was working on the hospital ward as a psychiatric aide, playing cards, administering simple medications, talking with and generally supervising the mental patients. Since they went to bed at 9 P.M., he had three hours to study—except for a 10:15 medication break—until his midnight quitting time. It was a convenient arrangement for getting through law school.

Busy as he was, Dick found time to date his first love, Janette, whom he had met at Indiana University. Her overpowering ambition was to marry him. For nearly three years she prodded and pleaded and prayed for the walk to the altar with Dick. And all the time he would carefully explain how important it was for him to finish law school and pass the bar examination. The situation begged patience.

But Janette could wait no longer and, in the words of Dick's stepmother, her decision "like to kill him." There would be many other women in his life, but none quite like his first great love. Only his dedication to law school stopped him. Dr. Bertrand Wechsler, one of his Valpo law professors who has since become a close friend, remembers:

I had him in one course in his last semester in school. I had him in a technical course which had to do with death taxation, gift taxation, etc. He sat near the end of the room in the corner by the window. I called on him once during class and somehow or other, his answer wasn't responsive. He didn't get quite on issue and apparently I put it out to him that his response somehow was less than satisfactory. It was the only time I ever talked to him. He got a "B" in my course, which is a very good grade in law school. "A's" are very rare; "B's" once in a while. About 75 percent of all grades are "C" in law school. He got a "B" in my course and I didn't know him, never talked to him, never had anything to do with him. Sometime later I ran into him at an NAACP Young Adult meeting. He was surprised to see me there. We talked and we got to know each other for a while about a few months later. He told me he thought I was the most racist professor we had out at Valparaiso and we had a lot of them. So I laughed. His feeling obviously grew out of our first exchange. We always kid each other about that. But then he was very quiet in law school. The school says he sort of came and went—very quiet, primarily on his own.

But Dick's quietness was deceptive. For at about this time he was caught up in Indiana's first restaurant sit-in. He and his friends, all well-dressed and well-known, occupied a booth in a Michigan City restaurant and ordered coffee. All they received from the waitress was a blank stare—no coffee, no explanation even.

But the next day they were served and their sit-in victory prompted other restaurants to follow suit. This was in 1958 when Dick, a twenty-four-year-old law student, debuted in politics as a Democratic primary candidate for Michigan Township Justice of the Peace. It had long since been a tradition that a black man hold at least one political office in Michigan City. For years, Dick's father had been quite active in politics, including driving carloads of black voters to the polls on election day. Often Dick had worked side by side with his father and in the process gained valuable know-how in the subtle nuances of politics. Now his father encouraged him to run for office.

Since Dick had no money to hire a staff, his campaign was largely a family affair with his father, sisters and brothers doing most of the necessary leg work. The only candidate in the field of ten with training in law, the only candidate actually qualified to be a Justice of the Peace, he nevertheless ended up fourth in the race, receiving 395 votes to the winner's 642. He had lost an election, but gained a first-hand introduction to the political process that would stand him in good stead later on.

When Dick graduated the next year (1959) from Valparaiso Law School he was once again confronted with the necessity of employment. But this time he would not have to contend with bigoted, white personnel managers as he had during his brief stay in Chicago. This time he would rely primarily on his own people. This time his sister Gladys, and others would steer him to Gary attorney Ben Wilson and East Chicago (Ind.) attorney Henry Walker. He would confer with the two men—both enthusiastic about his potential as a lawyer—and make the fortunate decision to join attorney Walker, fortunate because attorney Wilson was later to become involved in a widely-publicized scandal.

As a kid, Dick had earned as little as twenty five cents for a whole day's work collecting junk in "the Patch." Now as a law clerk for attorney Walker, he did not receive much more —about seventy-five dollars a month. It was not so much a salary as a little something to help defray expenses. He sacrificed salary so that he could be schooled in the practical side of the law. Like most graduates, he had come out of school with a head full of theory only. He did not even know his way to the courthouse, nor how and where to file a legal brief and other legal procedures. When he learned in September 1959 that he had passed his bar examination, attorney Walker began assigning him cases involving court appearances.

Attorney Richard Hatcher's very first important case involved a black teen-ager who had been accused of brutal assault by a Mississippi white woman. She claimed he had pulled abreast of her car in a service station and made an obscene suggestion. Then he fled the Mississippi town and ended up in Gary, where he was arrested. Mississippi authorities wanted him extradited. But in the hearing before Indiana's governor at Indianapolis, attorney Hatcher, who knew the boy's return to Mississippi would mean certain death, argued so persuasively he gained his release. The story, with the young attorney's photograph, was front-paged in the *Chicago Defender*.

He also attracted the attention of County Prosecutor Floyd Vance who hired him as a part-time, $5,000-a-year, deputy prosecutor in the Criminal Court at the county seat in Crown Point. Working three days a week, he argued every kind of case from traffic offenses to murders, robberies, and rapes. Since he was only a part-timer, he opened a Michigan City law office in 1961, struggled with clients who were either unable or unwilling to pay him, then closed shop after only a few months. It was only a temporary setback, because in 1963 attorney Hatcher became a candidate for the Gary City Council.

3. Getting It Together

3. Getting It Together

A N UNSUCCESSFUL CAMPAIGN for Michigan Township Justice of the Peace in 1958 had been Attorney Hatcher's political debut. Five years elapsed before he tried again for a political office—a post in the Gary City Council as a councilman-at-large (elected city-wide, rather than from a particular district). His candidacy was a dovetailing of his developing public career with the long and checkered history of Gary.

Sitting in the northwest corner of Indiana about thirty-five miles southeast of downtown Chicago, Gary is the largest of four cities comprising the Calumet region's industrial area along a fifteen-mile arc on the nipple-end of Lake Michigan. It was a child of the U.S. Steel Company whose board chairman, Elbert H. Gary, disclosed plans in 1905 to build the city and name it after himself. The company wanted a mill location midway between Minnesota's iron ore and West Virginia's soft coal. By July 17, 1906, Gary was incorporated.

Until then the area had been largely a neglected wilderness, some twenty-two square miles of muck and marsh humming with hornets and yellow jackets, a wilderness thronged with bears, deer, ducks, and geese. U.S. Steel had acquired the land so discreetly, one transaction involved a courier toting $1,300,-000 through the streets of New York in a handbag.

Then in March, 1906 the firm leveled the sixty-foot sand

dunes and brought in dark loam costing millions of dollars from Illinois. It carved out some 2,500 acres of open-hearth furnaces and slag heaps. It sifted two miles of the Grand Calumet riverbed, extended a water tunnel a mile into the lake and ninety-five feet underground and constructed a harbor to receive ships bringing ore from the Lake Superior region.

The firm's architects created a variety of designs for housing construction. The mills cost $85 million, but housing, which seemed trivial, was allotted $15 million. Within three years, five hundred homes were occupied mostly by mill workers recruited from Eastern and Central Europe. Many of their homes were one to three room, tar-paper shacks with outside toilets, communal pumps and no screens. Dogs, pigs, goats, chickens, and sometimes cows, shared many of the dwellings with their human occupants. By lending money to its employes, U. S. Steel promoted home ownership and thus guaranteed itself a reasonably stable work force.

Eventually the firm—headquartered in New York and Pittsburgh—built five major plants in Gary and, to protect its huge investment, controlled the city's government by placing company officials on the boards of the town's newly founded institutions.[1] They were, in other words, the founding fathers, the power holders, executors of private economic policies and authority symbols.

After World War I, a slow but steady stream of blacks seeking opportunity flowed into "the good work town" from the South. Continuing through the 1930s, their trek speeded up during World War II, largely because of employment opportunities in the steel mills, then producing at full capacity as part of the nation's all-out war effort. Along with this black migration into the city came Latin Americans, Mexicans, Puerto Ricans and other non-whites seeking economic oppor-

1. James T. Jones, "Political Socialization in a Midwestern Industrial Community" (University of Illinois doctoral dissertation, 1965) .

tunity. By 1930 some 17,922 or 17 percent of Gary's residents were blacks. Another 3,486 were Mexicans. As foreign-born families moved from the city's Central District to the North Side or found homes in the Glen Park neighborhood south of the Little Calumet River, blacks and Mexicans, the greater part of whom were in the lower-income bracket, moved into the tenements, basements and substandard houses formerly occupied by the foreign born.

From 1918 to 1932 Gary was enmeshed in "deals" between racketeers and public officials resulting largely from the illegal "bootlegging" of whiskey. According to political scientist James T. Jones:

> Indiana became a dry state on April 2, 1918 and 18 days later the first of many exposés of violations on the part of public officials of Gary took place—40 gallons of whiskey intended for a justice of the peace in the city were taken from a wagon in nearby East Chicago. The whiskey was being transported from Chicago (the vice capital of the United States).[2]

Jones continues:

> By 1922, the manufacture and sale of whiskey in Gary had reached such proportions that Gary became known nationally by the sequence of events which occurred commencing in August of that year. One hundred twenty-seven boot-leggers were arrested, and in January 1923, sixty-two persons were indicted by the federal government on charges of conspiracy to violate the federal prohibition laws. A number of public officials were charged in the conspiracy. Heading the list was Mayor Roswell O. Johnson, serving the second of his three terms as mayor; others included were the city judge, president of the board of works, a police sergeant, sheriff of the county, three policemen, the county prosecutor, a justice of the peace, a constable and three lawyers. Johnson received a sentence of eighteen months and a $2,000 fine; he was sent

2. Ibid.

to the federal prison in Atlanta, Ga., in April, 1925. Thus, Mayor Johnson became the second of Gary's mayors to be arrested, and the first to be convicted while in office.

This was not the end of Johnson's successes in politics, for after being released and pardoned by President Coolidge in March, 1929, he was again elected mayor of Gary in November, 1929, and by a substantial majority.[3]

The low turnout of voters in Gary's 1929 election suggested widespread disgust with political corruption. Indeed, until 1968, organized crime operated in apparent freedom. Numerous public officials used their offices to plunder rather than to build. Could the steel city, whose second largest industry had been vice and graft, be reformed? The question teased several young black idealists back in 1959 when Attorney Hatcher moved to Gary. Their consideration of that question was not a mere mental exercise, not an intriguing puzzle to be merely contemplated. The question begged action.

The young men, Attorney Hatcher, businessmen John Lawshe and Dozier Allen, county probation officer Houston Coleman, bus driver John Gibson and Attorney Jackie Shropshire, began meeting in Shropshire's office to map strategies that might implement their belief that Gary could be reformed. Sundays after church until about 4 P.M. they sipped cocktails and chewed over the problems confronting their city. These were informal bull sessions that in time would be formalized as they generated ideas that could form the nucleus of a new political program.

The inspiration for that program lay in Lawshe's intense interest in emerging Africa, an interest arising in part out of the fact that his sister-in-law was the wife of Ethiopia's Ambassador to the United States. Lawshe believed blacks desperately needed something to hold onto in the midst of their American ordeal. For him, that something was Mother Africa.

3. Ibid.

There was no other place in the world to turn for spiritual sustenance. Lawshe had been especially inspired by the Mau Mau whose bloody 1952–56 rebellion in Kenya eventually led to that country's independence under President Jomo (Burning Spear) Kenyatta. Early in his political career the bearded statesman had published *Muigwithania*, a newspaper named after the Kikuyu term meaning: "We are together."

It was inevitable, then, that the concerned young blacks would name their budding organization, "Muigwithania," to indicate they were together in their determination to reform Gary. As their meetings continued, they quietly recruited civic-minded persons who shared their point of view and within a year Muigwithania grew from six to forty members, many of whom were still college students. Even so, the organization was not "on the map" in the black community. It badly needed operating funds.

Muigwithania initially assessed its members one hundred dollars each, payable in twenty-five-dollar installments, and also borrowed one thousand dollars from one of its members who was a young doctor. But its major fund-raising efforts came from public dances which attracted thousands of young people. One of the organization's first big successes was a 1960, $10-a-plate, dinner-dance for Andrew Hatcher, press secretary to newly-elected President John F. Kennedy. Muigwithania had backed the young president partially as a consequence of the state-wide organizing efforts of Hatcher's first law partner, Attorney Henry Walker.

This political fund-raising was only a harbinger of things to come. It had been obvious to Muigwithania members that if they were really going to make a difference in the character of Gary, some of them had to enter politics as reform candidates. But the very mechanics of the city's political processes was going to make that a formidable undertaking.

Gary politics is based on precinct organizations which are

usually controlled by a single individual, the committeeman.
The elected committeeman appoints a vice-committeeman,
making a total of 262 persons for each party from the 131 precincts. These party committeemen may come together in the
districts to form district organizations and finally a city-wide
party organization. Both the Democrats and Republicans have
city-wide organizations with elected officials. In the case of the
Republicans, it is very difficult to maintain an organization
since it is often nearly impossible to attract persons to the
positions in every precinct. Very little is heard of the party organizations between elections and party activities, for the most
part, thrive on an informal face-to-face basis.[4]

Clearly, this was not a political setting inviting to such rank
amateurs as the members of Muigwithania. But what they
lacked in experience and political sophistication, they made
up for in with zeal and enthusiasm. One member, Quinton
Smith, now president of the Gary City Council, recalls:

> *They were all very green and of course I was too,
> except that I was a much older man. They all wanted
> to run for the big offices first. I said, "Can you take
> your precinct? Well, I don't see how you're going to
> get in office if you can't take your own precinct." I
> said, "I took mine. I'm not the precinct committee-
> man, but I take sides and I decide what happens
> there. I think that before you start running for state
> senator and for state representative, you should be
> pretty well sure that some people believe in you."*

It was reasonable advice, especially since Muigwithania was
not financially ready for major political campaigns. Even a
candidacy for such comparatively minor offices as township

4. Ibid.

trustee or assessor required a minimum outlay of five thousand dollars. Dozier Allen, now a city councilman, remembers:

> *At this time, the city organization had control of the precinct organization. I mean they had control of it! The machine would tell them to jump and they would say, "How far?" You couldn't get anything out of a precinct committeeman at all. So we figured we could bust them and then we could tell them what to do. We assumed if we got enough of these small offices, then the city organization would have to recognize us in terms of the big offices.*
>
> *But we didn't know at the time that the precinct organization was so tightly controlled by the city organization that if one of us supported someone not controlled by the machine then the precinct organization would simply chop up their campaign. In other words, suppose I'm supporting Dick Hatcher and someone else and the precinct organization says, "Okay, you drop Hatcher. If you don't, then we're just going to cut him out."*

Muigwithania's young idealists hoped they could change this sort of machine rule by aligning with some of Gary's veteran politicians. They had hoped for a test of this loose coalition in the 1962 election for state representatives. A delegation of union officials and politicians asked Attorney Hatcher, then Muigwithania's president, to enter the race and replace State Representative James Hunter, who had been the only black man in the legislature for most of the twenty-four years of his service. Hunter was being pressured to run for the State Senate. A victory for him would amount to a political promotion for Indiana's blacks.

But Hunter felt he could not win the senate post because

he was opposed by the mayors of two major Indiana cities—
Gary and East Chicago. Furthermore, Hatcher did not want
to run against Hunter for his State House seat, because he believed this would split the Negro vote and thus open the possibility of no black man in the legislature at all. Besides, they
had been good friends ever since the old pro took the rookie
under his political wings. On many an afternoon Hatcher
would visit Hunter and the veteran would say, "Come on,
let's go for a ride." And they would spend hours driving
around Gary and the county talking to people and making
important political contacts. Perhaps the old man had a pre-
monition that he was going to die within a year and was therefore anxious to groom his potential successor.

In any case, Hatcher's backers had organized a huge rally
at which he was slated to announce his candidacy. Instead, he
thanked them for honoring him, then explained his decision
not to run for state representative. But he was by no means
retiring from politics. Instead, he was preparing himself for
the bigger political roles that lay ahead of him. Resigning
his job as deputy prosecutor in the Criminal Court at the
county seat in Crown Point, he joined the Juvenile Court
staff in Gary and transferred his law practice from Attorney
Henry Walker's East Chicago office to the Gary office of fellow
Muigwithania founder Attorney Jackie Shropshire. It was
1963, a good year to enter the spring primaries for the Gary
City Council because not only did he receive 99 percent of the
black vote, he polled more votes (12,779) than any councilman-at-large in Gary's history. His victory in the fall general
election was routine, even though opponents attacked him re-
lentlessly for his longtime role as "a radical."

Hatcher did not forsake that role when he joined the City
Council. He still pressed for the reformist goals for which
Muigwithania had strived. Before his election he had distin-
guished himself in 1962 as one of the NAACP attorneys in

a federal law suit to end *de facto* segregation in Gary's schools. In hearings before the Gary Police Civil Service Commission, he had represented victims of police brutality. Now in the City Council he became the prime mover for passage of a fair housing law, having led a 1963 demonstration of some fifteen thousand people. His persistence resulted in the 1965 passage by the Council of the nation's strongest open occupancy bill. Councilman Hatcher's crusading also helped to integrate Gary's fire stations and the patients' wards and staffs of the city's two major hospitals. Within a year after his election he became council president, both the youngest and first freshman councilman to do so. But his successes did not go unchallenged. Opponents accused him of Communist leanings and claimed he had been a W. E. B. Du Bois club member while a student at Indiana University. He had not.

In February 1965, William J. Collins, who identified himself as the head of a citizens' rights organization, filed a petition seeking Hatcher's removal from the City Council. Submitted under rules which provide for removal of a councilman upon a misdemeanor conviction, the petition alleged Hatcher had six traffic arrests. It claimed he was fined $10 and court costs in 1961 for a speeding offense and that on five subsequent violations the charges were either dismissed or ignored. Collins also claimed Hatcher violated a written promise to appear in court on a December 1964 traffic violation. The councilman's reply to all of this was simple: the driving record cited in the petition was not his. The entire affair, he declared, had been part of a systematic effort to punish councilmen who had voted for civil rights legislation.

But Councilman Hatcher was not to be intimidated. Whether he intended it or not, he continued to make headlines as a civil rights crusader. By August 1966 the *Gary Post-Tribune* reported he was denying his candidacy for mayor about as often as he spoke on the City Council floor. The paper revealed a Committee of 100 had arranged a $100-per-person social affair that would raise $10,000 for Hatcher and thus give him convincing proof that he could get the necessary support to provide more than token opposition to the regular Democratic organization candidate in 1967. One of the arrangers of the fund-raising affair was Dozier Allen, a key person throughout Hatcher's burgeoning political career in Gary.

Only one year before the 1967 mayoral primary, Allen had demonstrated that an independent could run a strong race against the regular Democratic organization. With the support of Hatcher and other Muigwithania members, Allen had come within seven hundred votes of winning the May 1966 Democratic primary race for Calumet Township Assessor even though the Democratic machine had slated five candidates, including four Negroes, to divide the vote. Allen was also opposed by white incumbent Tom Fadell, with his own very substantial number of patronage workers, and by former Mayor John Viscloskey. An analysis of the election by Hatcher's former law professor, Dr. Bertrand Wechsler, indicated that Allen had lost the election in the township to Fadell but carried Gary with 10,011 votes. He had polled 27 percent of the Gary vote to Fadell's 25.8 percent. Allen, then, had been defeated primarily by the suburban vote.

His near-victory had clearly demonstrated that a black man could challenge the Democratic machine even for the mayor's office. So in the fall of 1966 a group of Gary school teachers headed by Jesse Bell, now Gary's City Controller, and Vernal Williams formed a society to draft Councilman Hatcher for the mayor's race. That his political stock was going up became even more evident in December when he was one of eight persons (including Cleveland mayoral hopeful, Carl B. Stokes) from across the nation invited to dine with Vice President Hubert H. Humphrey and discuss black disenchantment with the Johnson Administration which had shown it was not totally committed to ending segregation and poverty.

The association with Humphrey was going to prove politically invaluable later on, because Hatcher had definitely decided to challenge the Democratic machine in the party's May primary. If he won, then he would be well on his way to becoming Gary's first black mayor.

4.The Campaign Trail

4. The Campaign Trail

O N FRIDAY THE 13TH, Councilman Hatcher defied ancient superstitions and announced his candidacy for mayor. "Today, hopefully a new freedom movement will be born," he said in his January 1967 statement, "a movement which will eventually free this community politically from the shackles of graft, corruption, inefficiency, poverty, racism and stagnation."

Hatcher's momentous announcement overshadowed a gentlemanly quarrel he was having with fellow Muigwithania member Dozier Allen who wanted to run for the seat Hatcher would be vacating. The councilman contended the black community should focus all of its political energies on his mayoral effort rather than scattershoot for several offices. Allen, on the other hand, argued that the black community was politically sophisticated enough to throw itself into more than one race.

A public airing of their differences only pushed the two men further apart and the issue was stalemated with Hatcher employing the means and wherewithal he deemed necessary for his election and Allen doing likewise.

Allen believed their political differences reflected their dissimilar backgrounds. Gary had been his birthplace, while Hatcher had moved there only seven years earlier from Michigan City. A Garyite for thirty-seven years, Allen had grown with the city. He felt he could not enter Michigan City where

Hatcher grew up and know enough about its makeup to make
any reasonably accurate political judgments and certainly not
to run for any political office. Therefore, according to Allen's
reasoning, Hatcher should not be running for a Gary office.

Nevertheless, others had decided that Hatcher, despite his
relative newness to Gary, could make a significant difference
in City Hall if for no other reason than his courage and im-
peccable honesty. He had spurned a $25,000 bribe offer not
to enter the mayoral race, refused another $50,000 to with-
draw, and ignored yet another $100,000 offered indirectly
through one of his aides. "I was in a restaurant one night
when a guy opened a large bag loaded with dough," the aide
reports. "He wanted me or my partner to offer it to Dick. We
paid our checks and left. I had knots in my stomach for days.
It scared hell out of me."

Yet it was the sort of drama that inspired "Midtown,"
Gary's black community. Early in the election campaign there
were indications that black voters in all sizes, shapes, and previous conditions of political servitude were behind Hatcher.
They were rebelling against the Democratic organization
which had long controlled the ghetto vote through the usual
precinct network of block-level politicians, patronage, pay-
offs, "ghost" voting, and protection of Negro gambling operations. Gone now were the days when a Democratic organization candidate like incumbent Mayor A. Martin Katz could
come out of the all-black third, fourth, and fifth districts with
pluralities of several hundred in each precinct. Katz had
failed to carry a single white precinct when he was elected in
1963, moving into City Hall on the strength of black votes.
To attract blacks once again in 1967 he chose a black campaign manager, Lake County Coroner Dr. A. S. Williams and
a black speech-writer, Chuck Stone, former aide to Representative Adam Clayton Powell.

Even so, before the May 2 primary, black committeemen

on the city payroll found it almost impossible to recruit workers for their organization. Blacks were almost solidly behind Hatcher, the first black man ever to win the mayoral nomination either on the Democratic or Republican ticket in Gary. Yet in his campaign speeches, Hatcher admitted Katz had been "probably more fair" to blacks than any predecessor. He criticized the mayor's failure to consider qualified blacks for top jobs in the police, fire, and health departments and charged that nothing had changed during the prior three and a half years under Katz. "I ask you," he would question audiences, "are the slums any prettier? Are our schools any less crowded? Have they built one single public housing unit? Have they torn down one single building for urban renewal? Have they expanded the park system? Have they desegregated the schools?" Hatcher noted that blacks were more than 50 percent of Gary's population, but held only 28 percent of city jobs.

Katz answered that Hatcher was "a radical, extremist and advocate of black power." He warned voters that Gary's record of freedom from major racial violence would end with his opponent's election. So newsmen who pestered Hatcher about the charges wanted to know: What about black power? "If you mean burning down buildings and getting rifles to 'liberate' ourselves, I'm not in that category," Hatcher explained. "I favor pooling resources to improve the conditions of persons of color. I don't believe in separatism."

As the campaign entered its stretch drive, Hatcher addressed a pre-election rally attended by four thousand persons at Municipal Auditorium. He thanked singers Harry Belafonte and Oscar Brown Jr., World Heavyweight Boxing Champion Muhammed Ali and others for appearing on his behalf. In forecasting his election, he said, "Each and everyone of us will sing in unison in one huge chorus in one polling booth after another throughout the entire city." He added,

"May 2, 1967 will be a day we shall never forget. On that day, the citizens of this city will proclaim a declaration of independence. It will be remembered as the day that plantation politics died in Gary, Indiana. No longer will we be stampeded to the polls like a bunch of cattle by a cynical, corrupt political machine. Plantation politics is dead. The day the machine can come to us with satchels full of stolen and extorted money and buy our votes is, thanks to God, over and gone."

Hatcher not only survived Katz's last-minute attacks, he defeated him in the May primary mainly because 13,133 votes were siphoned off by segregationist businessman Bernard Konrady. Hatcher polled 27,272 votes—fewer than 1,200 of them white and three of every four black votes—to Katz's 17,190. Indeed Katz, who had been elected four years earlier on the basis of strong black support, failed to carry a single precinct among those reported in the black-dominated fourth and fifth districts. His message to Hatcher was a telegram saying simply: "The people of Gary have spoken. Congratulations on your apparent victory."

It was a stunning upset since none of the published straw polls, newspaper columnists or radio commentators in Indiana's second largest city had predicted Hatcher's victory in the primary. Against the affluence of a Goliath Democratic machine, its built-in campaign workers on city and county payrolls, its hundreds of paid part-time workers and years of hardnose experience in clubhouse and precinct politics, all this black "little David" had going for him was a shoestring $37,000 and a batch of untested volunteers.

The work of these volunteers, as much as anything, had brought the near-miraculous primary victory. Hatcher's press chief, Chuck Deggans, had organized a group of semi-professional women who called themselves the Shock Troops. Their job had been to organize the black community for the

May 2 primary. They had sent Hatcher literature to thousands of black people, had spoken on his behalf at black churches, lodges and fraternal orders and had carried leaflets and buttons. They had been a small group by comparison with the regular Democratic machine forces and their rallies had never been as well attended as those of the machine. Yet they struck a nerve. Black people seemed to have a need for what they were saying. Children took up the case for Hatcher. His picture went up in poolrooms. One well-known brothel had his stickers prominently displayed throughout its premises and white customers slowly dropped out of sight.

Meanwhile, the Republican primary was won by Joseph B. Radigan, college-dropout son of an Irish immigrant and proprietor of a downtown furniture store inherited from his family. He had received a quite small, but sufficient 3,846 votes in his first try for public office. Although Katz buried the hatchet and publicly endorsed Hatcher, many of his department heads began wearing Radigan buttons after the primary. Why would heretofore loyal Democrats back a Republican? An answer came swiftly in July 1967 when the all-Democrat City Council eliminated the jobs of the mayor's executive secretary and his clerk-typist from the $8.5 million budget for 1968. The budget passed by a 7 to 1 vote with Councilman Hatcher dissenting. "No one is fooled," he declared. "The budget was cut to cripple and hamper the operation of the city next year."

Nevertheless, Hatcher's team launched "Operation Saturation," a door-to-door effort to register eligible voters for the fall general election and thus bring about the sort of black political power that others had merely talked about. His team of two thousand volunteers (about 400 white) was a new breed—all young, enthusiastic, disciplined, all aware of how to run an election or be run out of it. Calculating closely, they knew they needed at least 10 percent of the white vote to help swing an election that otherwise might be next to impossible for Hatcher.

"If we had to do it all over again and knew the obstacles, maybe we wouldn't have tried it at all," campaign manager Henry Coleman admitted at the time. He had begun work on Hatcher's campaign eighteen months earlier. During that time few of Gary's black ministers or established black politicians jumped on the Hatcher bandwagon. "They didn't think we had a chance of winning," Coleman recalled, "and they didn't think the time was right. I told them it was now or never."

But was it? Many of Gary's whites had dramatically demonstrated their strong, anti-black sentiment when they helped Alabama Governor George C. Wallace defeat former Governor Matthew E. Welsh in Lake County by 42,712 to 40,185 votes in the 1964 Indiana presidential primary. Many others were quietly running to Gary's suburbs like medievalists fleeing the black plague. County officials told Hatcher they didn't think the people in Gary were ready for a black mayor. "Which people?" he wanted to know. "Thousands voted for me in the primary, and I think I can win the election in November. I'm not predicting a runaway election. It will be close. But I think I can win it."

The most important of the county officials Hatcher confronted was short, pudgy, shifty-eyed John Krupa, county clerk, county Democratic chairman, holder of the key posts of secretary of the County Election Board and secretary of the Board of Canvassers, middle-class extoller of the virtues of hard work and self-reliance, super-American patriot, passionate anti-Communist, a would-be social analyst who associated the American Civil Liberties Union with subversion and who applauded Gary's requirement that garbage collectors and all other municipal employes take loyalty oaths. He had once told Hatcher that he (Krupa) was Polish and the Poles had had to wait their turn to get power. "The trouble with you people is you're not willing to wait your turn. You're too impatient," he scolded with an "I-know-Negroes" tone of authority.

Immediately after Hatcher's upset victory in the Democratic primary, Krupa announced that Hatcher deserved and would receive full support from the county organization. Krupa also indicated his opposition to formation of a third party embittered by Hatcher's defeat of Katz and Konrady. It had been rumored immediately after the primary election that some high-ranking Democrats were considering such a move.

Krupa would have no part of it. However, he qualified his endorsement of Hatcher by insisting that the young councilman purge himself of a group of young campaign workers who Krupa decided were not good patriots. This had to be done, the chairman said, before he could commit the county organization to helping Hatcher. He indicated he was talking about what he called the "new radical element that [had] taken over the civil rights struggle from the old-fashioned, well-intentioned, proper-acting organizations like the NAACP." Krupa wanted Hatcher not to invite such "radicals" as Dr. Martin Luther King Jr. and Stokely Carmichael to participate in his campaign.

But it soon become clear that all of Krupa's talk about "radicals" was only a smokescreen for what he really had in mind. "After I won the Democratic primary in May," Hatcher recalls, "Krupa met with me and said he wanted to name the police chief and controller and several other key officers. And I told him, 'Look, too many people have worked too hard in this, and I'm not going to abdicate my responsibilities or sell them out. I'm going to name my own police chief and controller.'"

Reverting to his subterfuge, the Democratic chief demanded that Hatcher denounce specifically and by name Martin Luther King Jr., Stokely Carmichael, controversial folk singer

Joan Baez, H. Rap Brown and Marlon Brando, who, with other American liberals, had sponsored a "peace" advertisement in the London *Times*. Hatcher refused, leaving no doubt in anyone's mind about his independence of the party chairman. A mayor should demonstrate his independence before he is elected, the councilman explained, and not wait until he enters office to assert himself. Krupa responded by distributing a reprint of an alleged Hatcher interview in *Muhammad Speaks*, the Black Muslim newspaper. He was quoted as suggesting Hanoi should try captured American pilots as war criminals. Krupa did not publicize the paper's later retraction of the story and its admission that Hatcher had been misquoted. Although the retraction supported Hatcher's own denials, red, white and blue Radigan billboards blossomed all over Gary, proclaiming the Republican candidate "100 percent American" and thus inferring that Hatcher—whose ancestors arrived on these shores at least two centuries before Radigan's Irish forebears—was un-American.

Hatcher stoutly refused to discuss the war in Vietnam further on grounds that "the mayor's race is a local campaign and we ought to talk about what we are going to do right here in Gary. As for my denouncing Stokely Carmichael," he declared, "I've already said again and again I'm opposed to anyone who advocates violence. Krupa has a long list of people he wants me to denounce. And if I denounce them today, he'd have a whole new list tomorrow. He wouldn't support me if I stood on my head." The young fighter suggested, instead, that county Democratic leaders denounce George (Cha-Cha) Chacharis, one major Democrat who was backing Radigan. Cha-Cha had been Gary's mayor from 1958 to 1962, before being convicted of income tax evasion in 1963.

As for Krupa's charges that Hatcher was surrounded with pinkos, the nominee answered he wasn't accountable for the motives of all his supporters. "I'm certain I'll get a lot of votes from prostitutes," he said at the time, "but it is obviously unfair to hold me responsible for their attitudes or willingness to break the law. If the county chairman has any proof of subversion and brings it to me, I would be the first to act and disassociate myself from such people. No such evidence has been delivered."

Still Krupa persisted in his opposition to Hatcher. The extremist label he pinned on the Democratic nominee stuck, and was reflected in the cold reception Hatcher received on vote-seeking tours of supermarkets and shopping centers in white neighborhoods. Whites avoided him. Many refused to shake his hand. Sometimes in speeches to indifferent, even hostile white audiences, he would shock and, in a few cases, embarrass them by stopping abruptly and saying: "I know you haven't heard a word I said. All you see in front of you is black. But if by some miracle, race was ruled out and I and my opponent were considered only on qualifications, this election wouldn't even be close. All my opponent talks about is that he comes from an old family, long established in Gary. He says he's been in the furniture business forty-seven years. I want to see that he stays there."

Meanwhile, the Democratic organization reportedly offered twenty dollars to anyone who would tear down Hatcher campaign posters, although Krupa had claimed it did not have enough money to support the Democratic nominee. Angered by Krupa's vendetta, both Indiana Governor Roger D. Branigin and Gordon St. Angelo, Democratic state chairman, demanded he resign his party post. Krupa refused, claiming patriotism came before party loyalty. It was not a matter of the candidate's color, he insisted, a replica of the American flag fluttering on his tie pin. The only color he was worried about was "the red, white and blue," he claimed. He attacked

Hatcher's patriotism even though he knew Vice-President Humphrey and Senator Robert F. Kennedy had received satisfactory security checks on Hatcher before endorsing him.

By now the fight between Krupa and Hatcher troubled top national Democrats who feared blacks across the country would turn away from their party in 1968 if Hatcher lost the election. In June, he visited Washington, ate a White House dinner with President Johnson, met with Housing Secretary Robert C. Weaver and Labor Secretary W. Willard Wirtz and was assured of help from the Democratic National Committee. Still, as the 1967 summer wore on, Hatcher's campaign funds dipped to new lows.

Gary mayoralty campaigns usually cost more than a quarter-million dollars. Hatcher had cut his to the bone, but he still needed about $125,000 to pay for billboard signs, radio time, literature, and office rentals. He did not, of course, expect financial help from the Democratic machine. Krupa had refused his request for a loan or contribution with the claim that mayoral candidates had to raise their own campaign money. Yet he was later to admit granting a $15,000 loan to incumbent Mayor Katz for his 1963 campaign.

On August 4 came a showdown between Hatcher and Krupa at a three-hour meeting of the County organization. Hatcher opened his portion of the meeting by reading a four-page statement pledging to denounce anyone who advocates violence or overthrow of the U.S. Government. Then he went on to say: "As I see it, there are two basic reasons questioning my candidacy: First of all, I am a Negro. Secondly, at least some people in the regular Democratic organization are fearful of the effects on the organization of my nomination and possible election."

Hatcher indicated his willingness to work for the organization, but declared he was not willing to submerge himself in the organization and become swallowed up by it. He was willing to become a part of the organization, he explained, if it was willing to become a part of the times. Then he declared: "I cannot help but wonder about those who say they are suspicious of some of the people who backed me in my drive for the Democratic nomination. Have you ever asked a nominee why he accepted the support of the various Democrat officials who have been indicted or convicted of misdemeanors or felonies? Have you ever asked a nominee why he accepted the support of public officials who have served time in the penitentiary? It seems inconsistent, to say the least, that you should now be concerned for the first time with the background and beliefs of those who supported the Democratic nominee. But if you are really and truly concerned about that and if this concern is really not more shadow than substance, let me assure you that my support has come from people who are honest and conscientious in their beliefs and in their dreams for a better life in the United States. I urge you not to turn your backs on the same Negro community in Gary which has always supported the Democratic nominees. Very few of the men sitting in this room would be here without the wholehearted support of the Negro community in Gary. Now for the first time you are being asked to support for public office a man who has emerged as a winning candidate from that same community. If you fail him in that support, then no matter how you explain it, you will never be able to conceal the true reason for that failure. I acknowledge with gratitude the support I have received from local and county Democratic officials, both white and Negro, some of whom are in this room. They have always demonstrated the broad kind of political vision we all need more of."

While Hatcher's statement aroused an air of unrestrained excitement among Gary's liberals, it did not persuade the reactionary Krupa that he and the county organization should support the black mayoral candidate either with words or money. Meanwhile, Hatcher's financial situation was becoming desperate and called for desperate measures. He decided on a big gamble which his campaign manager was certain would waste money and which had been approved by his ten-man, campaign steering committee by only one vote. He inserted a $6,960 advertisement in the *New York Times* and another costing $860 in the *Gary Post-Tribune*. These expenditures left $14 in his campaign chest. At least three persons had mortgaged their homes to help raise money for the ads. The advertisement headlines read: "For God's sake, let's get ourselves together." The sixty-four-line text, surrounding a photograph of a white policeman clubbing a black man, went on to appeal for contributions from non-constituents across the country, as well as for an end to "bigotry . . . ignorance . . . violence." Within a week the advertisements had brought in some $9,000 in small donations—enough to cover the costs. Contributions ranged from one of $1,000 down to two 25-cent pieces wrapped in a note from an ADC mother who thought Hatcher needed the money more than she did. By October he had received about $60,000 in contributions.

Hatcher's impressive national showing only served to infuriate Krupa even more, as evidenced by his blistering speech at a Lake County Young Democratic Banquet attended by some 450 persons in East Chicago. The squat little County Chairman was only one of a dozen speakers on the program, but he was easily the most vituperative. "If I permitted the Gary takeover by leftists without a challenge," Krupa declared, "without calling this to the attention of the voters, I would place myself in the class of a Neville Chamberlain, who bent for Hitler's crowd."

Krupa added: "Gary will someday have a mayor who is a Negro and I hope I will be around to help in getting the job done. But in my book, he will have to be the kind of person who will not hesitate to repudiate the devil by name. Such a mayor will represent the best of all the Negroes and all the other people of Gary. He will be an American first."

In reading the prepared text of his talk, the County Chairman effectively dampened the social atmosphere at the banquet. He stood at the elevated podium as Hatcher sat directly below him only a few feet away. Heavy applause reverberated through the hall as he finished, but a later speaker, U.S. Representative Andrew Jacobs, an Indianapolis Democrat, won an even louder ovation. He explained he had been warned to avoid talking about the past troubles in Gary, but "my conscience and my heart dictate I shall enthusiastically endorse my fellow American Dick Hatcher for Mayor of Gary."

As the banquet ended, Hatcher told newsmen he had no immediate comment on Krupa's speech but termed ridiculous the County Chairman's statement that the breach with the county organization was planned by Hatcher. With all attention focused on him, the mayoral candidate was forced to hold an impromptu reception line as whites and blacks lined up to shake his hand and exchange words with him. Krupa, meanwhile, had left.

His vendetta against Hatcher was undoubtedly the main reason for a $25-per-person, fund-raising reception for the young candidate at the National Democratic Club in Washington, D.C. On hand at the two and a half hour affair, which reportedly raised $5,000 for Hatcher's campaign, were Senators Robert Kennedy of New York and Edward Kennedy of Massachusetts, former Senator Paul Douglas of Illinois and Vice-President Hubert H. Humphrey who, in a half-hour speech, appealed for Hatcher's election. Humphrey said he could not vote in the Gary election because he was not a Gary resident, but added: "I am the Vice-President of the United States and I know this young man. I have checked him out carefully. He will be the next mayor of Gary, Indiana."

Never before in his quarter century of public life, Humphrey continued, had he heard a man so succinctly, directly, and clearly, express the problems of contemporary times. Putting his arm around Hatcher, the Vice-President said: "The question before the citizens of Gary and the United States today is will we judge a man on his merit, character, experience, and willingness and capacity to serve or will we judge him on false charges." Then in a remark clearly directed to John Krupa, Humphrey declared: "It is the duty of the party, state and county, to back their candidate, particularly when they have a chance to make national history."

But as the November election approached, Krupa choose to make history in a different way. He ordered 5,286 names —most of them blacks—stricken from the voter registration rolls in Gary and added 3,000 whites who he alleged were new registrants. Now it seemed, Hatcher's defeat was certain. Yet, the same imagination which had inspired him to advertise nationally for campaign funds, moved him to make the second most important decision in his mayoral campaign. He filed a federal law suit against Krupa and the Lake County Democratic organization charging them with disfranchising black voters (in violation of the 1965 Voting Rights Act) and adding fictitious white registrants. He had filed it on "trick-or-treat" day, he explained, because he wanted all the tricks to occur on Halloween and not election day. Within a few days the U.S. Justice Department filed a similar suit as a follow-up to three weeks of intensive FBI investigation.

On the eve of election day, a three-judge federal court in Hammond, Indiana, convened for a single hearing of the Hatcher and Justice Department suits. Quickly, an FBI agent testified a twenty-two-man team he headed had uncovered 1,100 fictitious names, mostly in white areas. Other testimony revealed one way of padding the voter rolls had been to find a building and add a name for each window. A used-car dealer said a voter was registered to his lot although no one lived there. Another witness said she managed a fifty-two-unit apartment building in a white neighborhood and twenty-five voters were registered in the building who did not, to her knowledge, live there. Testimony disclosed some 4,620 bogus names had been registered in 60 precincts. Another 10,235 persons were not living at the addresses from which they were registered to vote in 160 of the county's 412 precincts.

The most damaging testimony came from Mrs. Marian Tokarski, a thirty-five-year-old Polish mother of three and a Democratic precinct committee woman who once denounced the NAACP and screamed at a housing meeting that blacks were not fit to live in her area. Her appearance now in court to admit her part in a brazen, widespread conspiracy to steal the election from Hatcher clearly indicated she had undergone a change of heart. She was ready to confess even though she risked a prison sentence on charges (later dropped) of conspiracy to violate Indiana's election laws. Nervously she blurted out she was "turning state's evidence" almost before she was sworn in before the court.

"They had me buffaloed into thinking Hatcher was a Communist and it was all right to do anything to beat him," Mrs. Tokarski testified. "But it got so I couldn't sleep any more. I thought of my husband (a gas station owner), my kids, and all my friends."

Back in the summer of 1967 she had known Hatcher was a reform candidate and had decided to support him despite the anti-black feelings that were intensifying in Gary's white areas. "I went to his office in July and told him I was on his side and that he could count on me," she recalls. Then Chairman Krupa came with his wild charges that Hatcher was "pinko" and "leftist" and began working openly for Radigan, the Republican mayoral candidate. Mrs. Tokarski began believing Krupa was correct. "I'm a Democrat," she thought, "but I am an American first." She phoned Radigan's home and informed his wife that she had decided to support the GOP nominee.

Weeks passed and tension mounted in the white precincts. Labor Day came and the campaign by now had become serious business. A few days later Mrs. Tokarski received a phone call from the Democratic organization in which she was asked "to beef up and fake names." But I was kind of leary and did nothing," she later told a newsman. Soon she began to hear reports from party members that the predominantly white district was the prime bargain area for a Democratic-Republican plot to steal the election for Radigan The organization, she said, was not convinced that backlash would suffice to elect Radigan in a city with a strong Democratic tradition and with black voter registration almost equal to the white.

Mrs. Tokarski received another party call, this time from a committeewoman who wanted to know what she was doing illegally to defeat Hatcher. The answer was, "Nothing!" The committeewoman persuaded her to come over immediately. At the woman's home, Mrs. Tokarski met another participant in the plot. They handed her fifty registration cards, signed with fake names, and told her to inscribe on the cards names that would not be easily described as fraudulent. She also agreed to urge one other party member, a committeeman, to join the plot.

Mrs. Tokarski was shocked when party contacts told her that ironworkers and prostitutes would cast the ghost ballots. Her shock deepened as she began to grasp the incredible scope of the scheme. "They were going to cast 14,200 votes for Radigan," she reported. "Hatcher would have been overwhelmed."

No sooner had she left the committeewoman's house with

the falsified registration cards than she began to regret what she had done. She began having trouble sleeping. Then three weeks before the election—"I was lying in bed and I kept saying to God, 'What am I going to do.' Suddenly I decided and then I slept."

Mrs. Tokarski had decided to tell Hatcher himself about the plot. "I felt I had the election in my hip pocket," she reported, "And I wanted to tell him I could do something about it. But I was real nervous." She began leaving messages at Hatcher's law office and began telling some of his associates that she had to see him. But in the turmoil of campaigning, Hatcher never received her messages. Finally in desperation, Mrs. Tokarski revealed her plans to a friend who advised her to contact a national magazine and have them set up an appointment with Hatcher. On October 23, fifteen days before the election, Mrs. Tokarski walked into the home of Hatcher's law partners and told her story to a staggered candidate.

"First I asked him if he really was a Communist," she later recalled in her report to the Chicago *Sun Times*. "So I told him the story and said if he didn't do something he would lose. When I told him they were going to steal fifteen to twenty thousand votes, he kept saying, 'That's fantastic! That's fantastic!'" Hatcher promptly urged Mrs. Tokarski to repeat her account to FBI agents and she did the next night at the same house. A few days later, she was interviewed by lawyers from the Justice Department's Civil Rights Division. The tide had turned.

For the next week and a half, Mrs. Tokarski had to be two-faced and act as if nothing had happened. "It was the hardest thing of all," she said. "At one time, they suspected me. One of them called and said that someone was poking around, and they had reason to believe I had talked and was getting a bundle. I said it wasn't true, and the part about the money wasn't. I guess it threw them off." Meanwhile, she failed to promote a Radigan meeting scheduled for her precinct and it turned out to be a flop.

But her testimony at the federal court in Hammond, Indiana, was the high point of the proceedings. The court ruled Krupa and the Democratic organization had indeed registered fraudulent voters, as Hatcher and the Justice Department charged, and had tried to disenfranchise thousands of black voters. Apologizing for not having time to make a more specific ruling thirteen hours before Gary's polls were to open, the court ordered one thousand false names removed from the voters' lists and sternly warned Lake County officials to obey the election laws.

Hatcher had won a battle but could still lose the war. To his chagrin, Indiana's Governor Roger D. Branigin had called out an estimated six thousand National Guardsmen to "drill" on election day at armories in towns minutes away from Gary. It was a maneuver that would cost taxpayers about $135,000. Loose talk of violence was fanned further by Mayor Katz who warned "force will be met with force." To Hatcher, these actions, allegedly designed to forestall violence, were in fact provocative, self-fulfilling prophecies of his defeat.

An already tense Gary ached now under the strain. Television newsmen, who had sought to build platforms for their cameras, complained that all the plywood in town had been sold to merchants anxious to board up their windows. Even Krupa relaxed his busy campaign against Hatcher long enough to phone his wife to see if workmen had boarded up the windows of his home in nearby East Chicago. And squads of city and state police nervously watched the black community.

Election day dawned crisp and cloudless. Councilman Hatcher arose at 7 A.M., breakfasted on bacon, scrambled eggs and toast and dressed himself in a dark suit, blue-striped tie and white shirt. Then he went to the Thorn School polling place in his 111th home precinct and voted. Surfboarding on the ever present wave of newsmen, he eased out of the polling place intending to head for his headquarters at a boarded-up building in a rough business area in downtown Gary's southern section. Almost immediately the crisp November air was alive with the clamor of black school children pulling on him, pounding his back, pleading for autographs. "All right! All right!" he said, permitting a wide grin to disturb his usually calm, intellectual, almost emotionless demeanor. But the children showed out, cut up and carried on. They shouted, "Hatcher! Hatcher!" They happily blocked the path to his car as if sensing he was going to be their mayor for real—in fact, the first black mayor in Gary's sixty-one-year history.

But there were circumstances working against that possibility. Some forty-six voting machines were reported mysteriously jammed in black precincts as Hatcher scurried about town in his telephone-equipped car to investigate. One of his precinct workers told him a call for repairs on a defective machine had been placed at 6:30 A.M. But repairmen did not arrive until four hours later. "When they left," she said, "we found the Hatcher label had been switched from the bottom position on the machine to confuse voters." Seven persons had used the machine before the switch was discovered. Another worker reported a Republican committeewoman had ordered Hatcher's poll watcher out of the polling place. Still another Hatcher aide complained: "They've been voting every stumblebum they can get in here." In a rare display of anger, the mayoral candidate promised privately: "If I lose this election, I'm going to let my hair grow long."

But his 2,000 volunteer workers were determined he was going to win. They had distributed voting materials around town and on election day drove some 200 cars to chauffeur voters to the polls. About a hundred of them saturated lily-white Glen Park and other Gary areas to serve as Hatcher's unofficial poll watchers. To Glen Parkers they were outsiders, hippies, and beatniks. Reports said they came from Illinois, Connecticut, Michigan, Ohio, New Jersey, California, and some Indiana cities. But one of their spokesmen described them as children of Gary parents, young people who were attending colleges and universities out of state.

In any case, by early afternoon on election day, the star witness in the federal court vote-rigging suit, Mrs. Marian Tokarski, had visited Hatcher's headquarters and tearfully recited a tale of threats against her life telephoned during the night. "If Hatcher wins," promised one caller, "you will never live to shake his hand!" When the harried candidate heard her plight, he rushed four of his security aides to her home to protect her.

Despite persistent talk of potential election-day violence, the overall 77,759-vote turnout easily wiped out Gary's previous record of 61,500 voters for the 1963 mayoral election. It represented about 42 percent of the 183,000 persons registered for the election. Observers contended, however, that part of that total included "ghosts," many of whom were apparently frightened away from the polls by the threat of possible federal contempt of court charges. The official count gave 39,812 votes (50.9 percent of the total) to Hatcher and 37,947 (49.1 percent) to Radigan—a razor-thin difference of 1,865 votes. Hatcher had received 13 percent of the total white vote, including 24 percent in one white Gary precinct. Radigan had gained less than 4 percent of the total black turnout. Hatcher had also led the Democratic ticket to victory behind him with the exception of two Council candidates who had failed to endorse him. Black political power, the fruits of hard work, had triumphed in Gary even though it would be two weeks before Radigan would concede the fact.

Arriving at City Hall at about 12:15 election night, after

sweating out election returns in his law office, Hatcher was met at the door by only a dozen white officials looking glum, sheepish, and frightened, a few offering polite congratulations. He was escorted to the mayor's heavily-carpeted, walnut-trimmed office where Katz small-talked about Mayor Carl B. Stokes's victorious Cleveland election, then invited Hatcher to try out for size the black, leather-bound, mayor's executive chair. But the Mayor-elect stood instead at the desk, absorbed with an almost monkish intensity in his note pad scribblings.

Meanwhile, in the City Council chambers off in another part of the building, a predominantly-black audience awaited a victory statement from Gary's new mayor. But he was unhurried, not out of arrogance, but because he had not received word of the official vote tallies from Krupa's office. He was extra cautious. Only the day before he had promised an enthusiastic supporter: "When I get elected, we're going to have the biggest inaugural ball this city has ever seen. We're going to serve soul food. You can believe that." But now there was a glimmer of a chance that there would be no ball. It was a sobering thought and Hatcher was not going to rush his moment of triumph.

Mayor Katz had phoned the county chairman and been told he would have the official vote tallies in about fifteen minutes. Hatcher waited. Krupa certified his victory only after consulting U.S. District Court Judge George M. Beamer of Hammond, a member of the three-judge panel which a day earlier had ordered Gary officials not to interfere with the conduct of a fair election. Even after the official word finally came, Hatcher still waited, reading and re-reading his three-page victory speech, occasionally penciling in a revision. As he passed, finally, through an anteroom leading to the council chamber, he even paused long enough to chat over the phone with the young son of a black City Hall official.

Now he was bathed in the glare of klieg lights, acknowl-

edging the roar from the packed City Council. "When you
went to the polls today," he declared finally, "you knew our
city was about to be strangled by the left hand of corruption
and the right hand of backwardness. You have broken that
grip and we plan to remake the city."

The room trembled as waves of sound richocheted from
wall to wall.

"The election showed that the Negro vote isn't for sale and
that a significant number of white voters no longer pay heed
to the old bugaboos about the danger of Blacks and Reds."

A loud amen gushed up from the audience.

"The victory presents an exciting challenge," Hatcher continued. "We shall lead the way for the whole country to follow. We shall prove that urban America need not wallow in
decay, that our cities can be revived and their people rejuve-
nated. Yes, we shall prove that diversity can be a source of
enrichment, that at least the people of one city in the nation
have decided, finally, to get themselves together."

Considering that Indiana's citizens voted 113,828 in 1850
to exclude blacks from settling in their state, considering that
Indiana has long been a Klu Klux Klan stronghold, considering that segregation in Indiana was not officially abolished
until 1949, the election of a black mayor for one of the state's
major cities was both revolutionary and a psychological boost
to practically all of Gary's black citizens. Mayor Hatcher
reported:

> It is hard to describe the type of pride felt by al-
> most every black person in the city of Gary. It may
> be no greater in children than in adults, but chil-
> dren are less inhibited in expressing it. They think
> this is a tremendous thing. We receive hundreds of

letters from children—some scrawled on a piece of paper, "We are glad, Mr. Hatcher, that you are our mayor." There is no measuring the inspirational factor in the fact that people got the job done and they did it themselves. They can go on to more difficult tasks with confidence. We need to organize and channel these energies into constructive action.

Later in a speech before a Hollywood, Florida, audience, Hatcher reminded them that this nation would not reach political maturity until black public officials had the right to fail as well as succeed. In other words, there was no reason to believe that they possessed the infallibility that many people expected of them. Having stressed his human-ness, the mayor-elect and his aides began organizing a $25-per-guest inauguration and Gary's first inaugural ball. The admission fee for the inauguration was Hatcher's substitute for the political cash assessment of city employes. Under previous administrations they had to kickback 2 percent of their salaries to a "flower and gift fund" for which the account book was maintained in the mayor's office. In addition, they were often required to buy $10, $25 and sometimes $50 tickets for political fund raising events. The fund had been used to entertain visiting dignitaries, for charitable contributions and political campaign expenses. But Hatcher, a long-time critic of the "flower fund," planned to use monies raised from his inauguration for charities and a mayor's scholarship fund.

On inauguration day, January 1, 1968, a siren-heralded motorcade delivered Hatcher to the back door of the City Auditorium. Inside, a crowd of fifteen thousand had been expected but bitter cold weather had reduced it to two thousand hardy folks who filled the main floor and strained for a good look at Hatcher and the other dignitaries seated behind a simple rostrum flanked by red and white flowers and patriotic bunting. Out in the audience was the mayor-elect's step-mother saying quietly: "I'm praying for God to keep bless-ing him."

And then came the time for Gwendolyn Brooks to read her poetic tribute to *Richard Gordon Hatcher:*

> Suddenly
> a Hand comes
> Help comes.
>
> This Moral Ceiling and Recurrent Giver—
> This Gymnast of the Fire
> made common sense into a Bread and fed
> the people—Said:
> Antiquity is not a proof of right.
> Said: Right must not be judged by candlelight.
> Above old fear, above old height and fibre,
> he is central candor, and a clarity.

And then came massive Judge James Parson of the Federal District Court in Chicago, berobed, words precise and tinged with excitement, giving the oath of office and a friendly hug to the new mayor. And applause lapsed into silence as Mayor Richard Gordon Hatcher announced the death of a close friend and dedicated the inaugural ceremonies to her memory. And then he delivered himself of his message:

> *My fellow Americans. Today we are witnessing a rebirth of Gary's determination to take its rightful place among the great cities of our nation. With a resolute mind we embark upon a four-year journey, to change the face of our city and unite the hearts of our citizens; to tear down slums and build healthy*

bodies; to destroy crime and create beauty; to expand industry and restrict pollution.

Gary, Indiana is a warm city—it has welcomed in large numbers into its midst emigrants from southern Europe, black people from the deep South and those who come from South of the border. In diversity, we have found strength; however, today is a new day. Let it be known that as of this moment, there are some who are no longer welcome in Gary, Indiana. Those who have made a profession of violating our laws—are no longer welcome. He who would stick up our businessmen and rape our women—is no longer welcome. Those who would bribe our policemen and other public officials and those public officials who accept bribes are no longer welcome and those who would sow the seeds of discord and peddle the poison of racism, let it be clearly understood, are no longer welcome in Gary, Indiana.

A special word to my brothers and sisters who because of circumstances beyond your control, find yourselves locked into miserable slums, without enough food to eat, inadequate clothing for your children and no hope for tomorrow. It is a primary goal of this administration to make your life better. To give you a decent place to live. To help create job opportunities for you and to assist you in every way in breaking the vicious chain of poverty. To give you your rightful share of the good life.

To our business community, including United States Steel Corporation and other large corporations, I say that Gary has been good to you, but it can be better. We assure you that this administration stands ready to support you in your efforts to rejuve-

nate our downtown, that it will work closely with you in attempting to attract new industry and enterprise in developing a healthy economic climate. In return, we shall ask you to roll up your sleeves and stand with us as we attempt to rebuild this city. Share with us your technical expertise, and your know-how and your money. Help us save our city. Each of you has a moral commitment to this community, and to your fellow man. And if you think so, now's the time to say so. There is nothing sacred in silence, nothing Christian in cowardice, nothing temperate in timidity.

To organized labor, we make a special plea that in the great tradition of your movement and out of your deep concern for the little man, the average man, you join us in this effort. Join us as we attempt to put into practice the great principles espoused by Samuel Gompers long ago and Joseph Germano more recently . . . "To every man his due."

To those who will be employes of this city, I say that the highest standards of integrity will be expected of you and anyone who fails to meet that requirement will be summarily discharged. Graft and corruption shall end and efficiency shall begin.

Today we have sworn in a new City Council. Represented there are men and women of integrity and great ability. I look forward to working closely with them for I am honored to call them all friend. Their responsibility is clear cut—to give to you the citizens of Gary four years of the finest, most progressive goverment in this city's history. To engage in constructive criticism and opposition to this administration when conscience so dictates, but never to oppose simply for opposition's sake. Our city is

*suffering. And unless the right medicine is adminis-
tered, it may die. We have long since passed the
point where either this administration or this Council can afford the luxury of playing politics with the
lives of our people.*

*To the press, we ask your understanding, patience
and help—all of our judgments shall not be correct,
but they shall be honestly made. You have a responsibility not only to report the news accurately, but
to interpret it with restraint.*

*Let me for a moment speak to our young people.
Your city needs you. We shall seek ways to capture
your spirit, imagination and creativity in order that
they may be true assets in our city's fight to improve
itself. Our future depends upon the dedication of
our young people today.*

*And finally, to all of our citizens, whether you live
in Glen Park, in Midtown or in Miller, I make a
special appeal. We cannot solve our problems, we
cannot save our city if we all are divided. The great
promise of our city will not be realized until we treat
each other as equals without respect to race or reli-
gion. To quote our president, "Until justice is blind
to color, until education is unaware of race, until
opportunity is unconcerned with the color of men's
skins, emancipation will be a proclamation and not a
fact. The Negro today asks justice. We do not answer him when we reply by asking patience." We
have talked long enough in this city about equality.
The time is here to live it. If we really want good
government, peace and unity, now's the time to practice what we preach. Good government comes in as-
sorted colors and nationalities.*

Together, we shall walk through our valleys of

*hope; together we shall climb the steep mountains
of opportunity, for we seek a high and beautiful new
plateau—a new plateau of economy and efficiency in
government, a new plateau of progress in government: a new plateau where every man, democrat and
republican, rich and poor, Jew and Gentile, black
and white, shall live in peace and dignity.*

*And so my fellow Americans, as we go from this
place, let us understand clearly our role and responsibility. This is a God-given opportunity to become
builders of the future instead of guardians of a bar-
ren past, and we must not waste it. Let us pray for
this wisdom and guidance. Let us dare to make a
new beginning. Let us shatter the walls of the ghetto
for all time. Let us build a new city and a new man
to inhabit it. Let each and everyone of us have the
courage to do what we all know must be done. For
we here in Gary, Indiana have much to say about
what will happen in urban America.*

*Our problems are many. But our determination is
great and we feel as Tennyson must have felt when
he said:*

Oh yet we trust that somehow good will be the final
goal of ill. . . .
That nothing walks with aimless feet
That not one life shall be destroyed
or cast as rubbish to the void

When God hath made the pile complete
Behold, we know not anything
I can but trust that good shall fall
At last—far off—at last to all
And every winter change to Spring.

And every Winter change to Spring. In Gary, together, we seek to change all winters to Spring. We know the way is difficult, but that does not discourage us. One of America's outstanding black poets, a scholar and a wise man, Professor Arna Bontemps, once wrote the following:

> We are not come to make a strife
> With words upon this hill;
> It is not wise to waste the life
> Against a stubborn will
> Yet we would die as some have done,
> Beating a way for the rising sun.

Gary is a rising sun. Together, we shall beat a way; together, we shall turn darkness into light, despair into hope and promise into progress. For God's sake, for Gary's sake—Let's get ourselves together.

5. Mayor Richard Gordon Hatcher

5. Mayor Richard Gordon Hatcher

THE GARY to which Mayor Hatcher was newly elected, had been built by the United States Steel Corporation sixty-one years earlier on the sandy, southern tip of Lake Michigan, then moulded into a company town. Soon its skyline was dominated by the huge smokestacks of mills bustling with Croats, Poles, Czechs, Slovaks, Serbs, Hungarians, Greeks, Italians, in short, some fifty-four different ethnic groups. The first blacks had come at the end of World War I. By 1968, 100,000 of them (56 percent of the population) had been squeezed into an area of only 6.6 square miles, though the city sprawls over 56.2 square miles. Throughout his campaign Hatcher had always said he wanted to become "mayor of all the people," that he would not show favoritism to blacks. Yet he had insisted his people had been "suffering, getting the short end of the stick in every phase of life." One proof was an Indiana State Civil Rights Commission study which revealed blacks accounted for only 28.2 percent of all city employes, despite their numerical dominance in Gary's population. They were in lower-paying jobs and held only two of thirty department-head posts. Of two hundred firemen, only sixty-two were blacks. Of two hundred and seventy-six policemen, only thirty-four were blacks and none held a captain's rank. Out of forty-two Indiana cities, Gary ranked thirty-fourth in the municipal employment of blacks. This situation represented the rankest kind of discrimination, despite any speeches the Katz administration could have made.

Moreover, the crime syndicate had found a cozy haven in Gary for years. Prostitutes, charging $20 to $100, worked in shifts to avoid occupational fatigue. With the syndicate's gross topping a billion dollars a year in Lake County (according to Northwest Indiana Crime Commission estimates), some elected officials made corruption a way of life. A "cooperative" mayor could expect an extracurricular income during his four-year term of from $3 million to $6 million—for doing nothing. His only real mistake would be to fail to report his graft on his income tax as had two recent mayors later convicted of income-tax evasion. Hatcher's predecessor, A. Martin Katz, a reform candidate in 1963, had pleaded that "You can't change established patterns of ten, twelve, thirty or forty years overnight." And Gary's police had made little effort to do so. Before the 1967 mayoral election, a Roman Catholic priest said he felt sorry for whoever won. As far as he could see the city could not be cleaned up in one, five, or even ten years. Not only was crime and corruption rampant, Gary was a city whose natural beauty had been pillaged and natural elements polluted.

Into this sordid picture, then, stepped Richard Gordon Hatcher, unburdened by political deals, so Spartan he neither smoked, drank nor used profanity, so dedicated he worked fourteen to eighteen hours a day, so religious he prayed in church on New Year's Eve while others partied, so committed his Gary soul brothers saw him as "a beautiful, black 'together' cat." In his new job he would be working for $20,000 a year —a $12,000 drop from his 1966 law practice income. He had pleaded in his victory speech: "Let's now transfer our campaign slogan, 'Let's Get Ourselves Together,' into action and make Gary a new and human city."

Hatcher was mayor now of a city which in many ways was a microcosm of the problems besetting urban America. It was hampered in coping with these problems, partially because it could not strengthen and organize strategic administrative and policy functions fast enough. "We can never be what we must become until we face up unflinchingly to what we are," the new mayor would soon declare in his first State of the City address. "Not in self-pity, not in despair, but in the pragmatic spirit of those who examine the real world in order to change it. Let us take a good hard look at the magnitude of the problems we face."

The problems were complicated by several factors, some old and some new, some common to many communities, and some perhaps unique to Gary.[1] In the first place, an intricate and confusing division of responsibilities among city officials prevented efficiency and confused accountability. Secondly, Gary had no civil service system. Instead, all local government positions, except elected ones, were filled by the patronage system. Thirdly, Gary's sordid history of organized and unorganized crime, graft and corruption so lowered the morale and so generated apathy among its citizens that most felt powerless to do anything about local problems. Fourthly, the city lacked strong citizens' or community groups directly focused on local good government needs or mobilized to provide support to new, improved governmental services. Fifthly, Gary's low salary scale made it difficult to recruit the sort of experienced, top-quality personnel necessary for efficient and flexible urban management. Finally, the highly industrialized city was hamstrung by an archaic, agrarian-oriented state legislature. Thus, for example, Gary had limited taxation powers. In addition the local poverty program was administered by the county, complicating tremendously the city's ability to

1. See "A Proposal to the Ford Foundation from the Mayor and Common Council of the City of Gary, Indiana," February 10, 1968.

deal effectively with problems of the poor within the city. Furthermore, the inherent tensions between county and city were heightened by the political and racial frictions that arose out of Mayor Hatcher's turbulent election campaign struggles with John Krupa, the Lake County Democratic chairman.

These, then, were a sampling of the problems the new mayor faced when he moved into his City Hall office for the first time at 10:30 A.M. on January 2, 1968. The city's General Fund held a scant $15,000, a sharp contrast to the $400,000 to $500,000 year-end balances usually left to city administrations in the past and also a sharp contrast to the $95,000 that would be in that Fund a year later. Nevertheless, Hatcher had come to head an urban laboratory which, because of the limited size of its problems by comparison with say New York or Chicago, was ripe for experimentation and innovation which could be quickly evaluated.

Unfortunately, because a black mayor was now in City Hall, many blacks and whites expected miracles. Indeed, during his first week a visiting group of black citizens demanded to know why all blacks did not have jobs and why all of Gary's slums had not been eliminated. They were soon to learn that efforts to deliver services were severely hampered in the administration's early days because equipment was in deplorable condition, much of it having been deliberately sabotaged by departing city employes. An intensive program of salvaging and rehabilitating equipment had to be instituted in several departments including most notably General Services (sanitation, etc.) and the Police Department.

While Mayor Hatcher was ill-equipped to perform miracles, his mayoral powers were such that he could hire and fire all city department heads and the deputies of certain other elected officials. As dispensers of all city jobs except those of policemen and firemen, previous mayors had been ruthless political bosses of self-serving political machines. If Mayor

Hatcher wished to head such a machine, he was going to have
to build it almost from scratch. A substantial number of his
predecessor's city hall staff left so abruptly, the new Mayor
had to find replacements immediately for tasks as routine as
manning the switchboard. And these replacements, many with
no prior administrative experience let alone city hall know-
how, had to learn on the job by trial and error.

Yet whenever Mayor Hatcher recruited personnel outside
of Gary, he was subjected to bitter criticism. Many of his local
supporters had expected him to turn over city jobs to them—
the usual reward for political services. But he was forced to
reckon with the grim fact that the sort of expertise he needed
so desperately was not always available locally. And he was
steadfast in his determination to appoint on the basis of occupational merit rather than meritorious services rendered
during the election. He was also determined to retain employes from the previous administration who, in addition
to wanting to remain on board, showed themselves to be honest and competent. "Dead wood" had to go, however. Included among the deposed was a former mayor who had been
kicked out of office for misuse of funds and promptly put
back on the city payroll by his successor. Charged with determining the capabilities of staffers in each of the city's departments was a Department of Program Development, established for the first time in Gary's history and headed by a
recent graduate of Yale University Law School, Edward
Grier. His responsibility was to troubleshoot for weaknesses
in the structure and personnel of each department and to
make recommendations that might bring about uniform quality throughout city government. Grier reports:

> *In all the investigations of city departments, I have
> started with the assumption that anybody who is
> held over from the previous administration, that is*

*to say, anyone who has had a city job prior to Jan-
uary 1, 1968, is a crook. That seems, by and large,
to have been a reasonable assumption. A large proportion of them were crooks and they have raped
the city. They have extorted every penny from it.
The municipal services are abysmally poor for a
city of this size and everything was done by political
deals and corruption in the most old-fashioned, clas-
sical, muck-racking period sense. This was tied in
very closely with organized crime and it seemed to
have been an "I'll-scratch-your-back-if-you'll-scratch-
mine" arrangement. Mayor Hatcher broke completely with this tradition to the point where many
of us think that if anything he has been too prin-
cipled and too unequivocal in the matter, too hard-
nosed and unyielding. But his thinking is that it is
necessary that this absolute position be taken because any compromise would be a sign of weakness
and, therefore, compromise is not really possible. He
felt he didn't have the maneuverability which a later
administration may have, that in a sense he was attempting to establish a Black Power beachhead in a
very hostile environment and this called for extraor-
dinary measures.*

The organization of Grier's Department of Program Development was only one of Mayor Hatcher's immediate administrative changes aimed at making Gary's government operate
more efficiently. Perhaps his most important administrative
innovation during his first year involved the reorganization of
the chain of command within the city. A cabinet replaced
an obsolete management system in which more than thirty
department heads reported directly to the Mayor. These departments now worked together under three "super-admin-

istrators" who were responsible for Gary's overall operations and problems in the areas of (1) public safety and law enforcement, (2) housing and community development and (3) fiscal and personnel administration. These super administrators were broad policy makers who were answerable only to the mayor. In this way, Hatcher created a more orderly flow of work and priorities.

Even so, he knew at the very outset that the long-run success of his administration heavily depended on the cooperation of absentee business ownership, particularly U.S. Steel. The giant corporation, headquartered in far off Pittsburgh and New York, had five plants in Gary employing about 65 percent of the city's work force. For many years Gary's "Big Daddy" had discouraged the entrance of other industries in order to protect its own labor market. Although it no longer actively pursued this course, the pattern had been set. Some smaller industries had come into the city, but it was still a U.S. Steel town. Again, Grier recalls:

> *The corporation has played a basically reactionary role in the city. Gary has one of the highest air pollution rates in the country, and although the U.S. Steel Corporation is not the sole cause of that—there are also oil refineries out in [nearby] Hammond and the other steel mills in the area—they certainly contributed. The agreement they signed with the city [in 1965] under the previous administration regarding their promise to set up air pollution control apparently was not nearly as favorable to the city as it ought to have been.*

In other words, although U.S. Steel provided work for more than 30,000 Garyites, it also dumped 36,000 tons of soot on the city each year and thus helped create an air pol-

lution problem which gave Gary the highest incidence of
tuberculosis in the country. The firm could point to its new
"BOP shop" (a basic oxygen process that scrubs waste gases
with water) and its "floculator clarifier" (a device that removes
emulsified oil wastes from water before returning it to the
lake). Theoretically, at least, enough such devices could null-
ify 90 percent of the steel mill's pollutants—but the cost
made that unlikely to happen. U.S. Steel had, however, promised the city to clean up most of the mess by 1972.

In the coming months, Mayor Hatcher was going to be concerned not only with the firm's pollution control but also its
failure to pay a fair tax to Gary. For years U.S. Steel had been
making millions of dollars worth of improvements in its Gary
facilities, yet its tax assessments kept going down. Again, Grier
comments:

> *Here's Gary, Indiana, which is one of the richest*
> *communities in the country in terms of the kinds of*
> *heavy industry which are located in it, and it's a poor*
> *town. The municipal service is inadequate and there*
> *just isn't enough money and it's clear that the cor-*
> *poration is grossly underassessed. Rumor has it, and*
> *I suppose it's true, that tax assessors retire as wealthy*
> *men because they're paid off. That, of course, I*
> *couldn't prove, but it is clear that the corporation*
> *just doesn't pay. And as a result of not paying its*
> *fair share all the services in the city are inadequate.*
> *They're assessed at $137 million. Assessment is sup-*
> *posed to be one-third of true value which would*
> *mean that their true value is supposed to be about*
> *$400 million. But the estimates I have heard range*
> *between one and two billion dollars. No one knows*
> *really how much their property is worth.*
> *The Mayor has initated an effort to see about*

the possibility of their being re-assessed. What the powers of the city government are in that regard is very unclear, because the power to set taxes is basically set by the township assessor who is an elected official and not appointed by the Mayor. But there is some obscure statutory language that has never been tested in court which seems to imply that the city controller has the power to look at the books of different property holders in the city and add anything which has been left out of the tax rules. The Mayor has already started some steps in that direction, but they are confidential. It seems clear that the corporation is not at all interested in having its property assessed at a higher value than it is at present.

While Mayor Hatcher tooled up for negotiations with U.S. Steel involving millions, he also confronted the first major staff crisis within his administration, the revolt of his $16,500-a-year corporation counsel, Hilbert Bradley. The two men had attended the same law school, but Bradley had been the school's first black graduate years before Hatcher's entry. Both had run for the city council in 1963, but only Hatcher won a councilman-at-large post. Bradley had failed again in 1967 when Hatcher was elected mayor. The older lawyer had campaigned for himself and for the mayoral candidate. He believed the time was right for a black mayor, that Hatcher would make a good mayor because of his intelligence and outstanding record as a Gary councilman for four years. Bradley recalls:

When he became mayor, I was in Birmingham, Alabama, and when he decided he was going to se-lect his employes, he phoned me and asked me if I had considered becoming a part of his administration. I told him that there had been several people who had contacted me concerning my becoming corporation counsel, but I hadn't given it too much consideration because I hadn't had an opportunity to talk with him. And so to make a long story short my request to him was a promise to the effect that I would be able to work on a part-time basis, the job paying $16,500 a year, which is not adequate compensation for a full-time corporation counsel. He agreed to that. My second condition was that I would be permitted to select my own staff. The implication was that I could select my own staff. I came back to town and was sworn in about three days later.

When we were in the process of selecting a person to become City Attorney, it was the first time that I came to the realization that the Mayor wanted to be consulted on the appointments for the office of corporation counsel. Since I had selected all the other employes, I decided that maybe I would compromise my position. The Mayor's suggestion was that he would designate three people from whom we would select one out of the three for the two additional appointees that were supposed to be made.

I needed help immediately because I had about 327 cases and I needed lawyers, seasoned lawyers. I only had at that time two other lawyers on my staff other than the Corporation Counsel and the City Attorney. Four lawyers to handle 327 pending cases. I was quite anxious to get two additional appointees. Well the Mayor has some kind of psychosis about delegating authority and as a result for about two months I was without these appointees and finally I *had gotten to the point where I went to the Mayor and told him that I simply had to have these appointees. Again he said he would give me the names of three lawyers from whom we in turn could select our two lawyers—people who would be qualified to do the job. Then he said something that carried with it the implication that I could go out and appoint two people.*

But the Mayor turned down the two men I recommended. This indicated to me that it was going to be his way or else and of course, being the kind of independent lawyer that I am, I decided that the best thing for me to do was to turn in my resignation. If I resigned, there was a possibility that I would shock him into the realization that he was going to have to delegate some authority if he was going to get the job done.

The resignation was to the effect that I was to resign on the 14th of January 1969 or as soon as the Mayor could retain a replacement. During the interim, I decided to go down to Washington for Rev. Abernathy's Poor People's Campaign in May 1969. I went by plane with a delegation of fifteen. When I returned to Gary, at least one of the Republican councilmen took the position that my pay should have been docked for the day that I was down in Washington. Newsmen also discussed the matter with the Mayor and he took the position that he thought it was not city business and my pay should have been docked. Naturally I became infuriated, because I thought that the Mayor would be the last person to say that my pay should be docked. I had had this phone conversation with him in Birmingham in which I agreed to take the office only if it was on a part-time basis. My being off one day, after working four to six hours a day and more, was more than compensating for the money that they were paying me.

And so in apparent retaliation to what he believed was a "knifing" from the mayor, Bradley made the sensational announcement to the newspapers that he was going to issue warrants for the arrests of any politicians who still had old campaign posters pasted up in public places like, for example, a board fence around a construction site or an empty store-front window. The list of people he promised to arrest included Senator Robert F. Kennedy, and Mayor Hatcher. Within thirty minutes after the startling announcement, Bradley received a letter from the mayor saying simply that his resignation was reluctantly being accepted immediately. In response, Bradley declared: "You might say that this is what I expected. All dictators react the same way whenever they cannot have their own way. It is either rule or ruin."

Mayor Hatcher had not expected to please everyone when he took office. He had, however, planned a vigorous attack on Gary's massive problems of unemployment, housing, crime, etc. For this purpose he received a series of special grants and consultative services. Among them:

> **Ford Foundation** granted $70,000 for studies in law enforcement, housing, and air pollution and $100,00 more for employing three special assistants to the mayor to help in the areas of housing, law enforcement and personnel administration and finance.
> **Potomac Institute** of Washington, D.C., loaned a top level administrator to the city for the first six months of 1968 to assist in establishing an administrative management system and developing programs.

Metropolitan Applied Research Center (MARC) of New York gave technical assistance in setting up office procedures; established contacts with foundations and aided in several funding endeavors.

Field Foundation awarded a $34,000 grant to AFDC mothers to organize welfare recipients.

Office of Economic Opportunity gave a $32,000 planning grant to set up Metro Corps, Inc., Gary's anti-poverty agency.

University of Chicago Center for Urban Studies assisted in resolving special problems.

Gary Model Cities received consultation services from numerous government and private agencies and industries including the federal departments of Health, Education and Welfare, Housing and Urban Development, Transportation, and Agriculture; Indiana State Department of Health; Purdue, Indiana and Illinios Universities; Gary School City; United States Steel and Portland Cement Association.

Labor Department furnished a program-planning expert to lay the groundwork for the Concentrated Employment Program.

Cummins Engine Foundation financed a nationwide talent search to attract highly qualified individuals to positions with the city administration.

This mix of federal government, corporate, and private foundation assistance produced immediate changes in Gary. In his first few months in office Mayor Hatcher could point to the $2.6 million Concentrated Employment Program (CEP) sponsored by the Department of Labor to train the otherwise unemployable. A controversial spinoff from CEP was the now-defunct Soul Inc., a federally-funded organization designed to take youth gang members and channel their energies into constructive activities such as operating their skating rink and movie theater. One of the more controversial aspects of the program had been its use of persons with prison and jail records. "I tell critics that we really have a choice," Mayor Hatcher explained at the time. "We can ignore the youth gangs and leave them to their own destructive impulses or we can work with them and try to reform them. I prefer doing the latter."

When the new Mayor took office, more than 80 percent of Gary's housing was substandard. Indeed, 40 percent of it was so substandard it was condemned. Although blacks accounted for 56 percent of the city's population, they were jammed into one-fourth of its dwelling units. Of these units, one-fifth failed to meet existing city building codes. No public housing had been constructed in Gary between 1952 and 1968. Part of the problem involved the unavailability of land. Housing developments to the North were prohibited by the steel mills and Lake Michigan, to the East and West by corporate limits. Further growth to the South required annexation. To attack this situation, the city undertook more than $10.5 million worth of inner-city urban-renewal projects and the Federal Department of Housing and Urban Development set a target of $2.6 million for a model-city program in 1969.

Gary began constructing 1,600 low- and middle-income housing units. U.S. Steel financed 500 additional units of middle-income housing. At the same time the city building department began aggressive enforcement of building code statutes. Department inspectors checked 4,184 buildings in one month for possible violations. (The previous administration for the same period had only been able to check 331 buildings.) Formerly, many building contractors had not even bothered to obtain building permits. Large companies would simply pay one flat fee and the building department was unable to determine how many jobs were handled under the one payment. Hatcher stopped the practice. Henceforth, everyone had to comply with the law.

Absentee landlords who refused to repair their property soon found the city boarding up their buildings and billing them for the costs. Those landlords who failed to repair buildings that were dangerous or unsafe for occupants had their properties seized through city court suits. Their rents were collected and the monies used to make necessary repairs, their only concern being the mortgage payments.

In July, 1968, the Hatcher administration launched Operation Showcase, a project designed to take a city block and show what could be done with only local governmental resources. If it needed garbage pickup four or five times a week to keep its alleys clean, the service was granted. If the block's residents needed house paint and could not afford it, the city supplied it. City Hall's concentrated interest in the one block soon inspired residents to take better care of their property.

But more important, Operation Showcase demonstrated that the city government was not some remote abstraction. This lesson was reinforced by the Mayor's Access Program (MAP), a deliberate effort to dispel the cold image of an impersonal, uncaring and unresponsive government. Six MAP teams were organized—one for every district in the city. These teams held meetings in neighborhoods all over the city (1) to give citizens a vehicle for their grievances and (2) to give city department heads a chance to explain programs under way in their departments. Thus MAP helped citizens feel closer to government. One woman reported she had been complaining to her landlord about conditions in her apartment and he had always ignored her. And then she told him she was going the next day to a MAP meeting where the Mayor was going to be present, and she was going to bring it up on the floor. That next morning he had repairmen out to her apartment.

Meanwhile, ground was broken for a $14 million, 300-room, Holiday Inn adjacent to City Hall. Mayor Hatcher hoped the Inn would help Gary become the convention center of Northwest Indiana and, for the first time in the city's history, he established a convention bureau. If Gary attracted large, national conventions, they would stimulate the city's economy.

To give black businessmen an opportunity to develop a greater involvement in Gary's economic mainstream, Mayor Hatcher secured a $737,000 grant from the Labor Department to organize a coalition of black contractors who instead of dealing with $20,000 and $30,000 jobs as individuals could, as a group, bid on multi-million dollar projects. The grant enabled the contractors to conduct a training program to improve and expand their businesses. Almost immediately they were able to share in a $4 million demolition contract let by the Gary Redevelopment Commission.

Initially, the entire contract had been earmarked for the National Wrecking Company in Chicago, the mayor discovered. Intervening with the U.S. Department of Housing and Urban Development and the Gary Redevelopment Commission, he argued vigorously that there was no way to rationalize a white contractor receiving $4 million to tear down black homes in the middle of the black community. Housing officials agreed and the black contractors eventually shared about $1 million of the $4 million contract.

Perhaps Mayor Hatcher's most important effort during his first year of office involved his intensive war on crime. Some gambling dens, after-hours drinking spots, and vice operations closed shop when he took office early in January 1968. Within a week after his inauguration there were police raids on gambling establishments and vice dens. Most of the crooks got the message and departed for friendlier environs. To convince the others, the athletic young Mayor accompanied a police raid in February on the Venus Cafe, the most lavish and notorious brothel and gambling center in town. "We want the citizens of Gary to know where the mayor's office stands on this sort of thing," Hatcher said to explain his personal participation in the crackdown.

He ordered police guards on city buses which had suffered thirty-one holdups in eleven months. When the mayor took office, Gary had only eight squad cars in working condition. Resigning officers had cannibalized many cars for parts. Very quickly the police force was furnished with forty-five squad cars.

As chief of the 276-man police force, Hatcher appointed forty-one-year-old James Hilton, a department veteran who had headed the narcotics squad for twelve years. Clamping down on organized crime, the new chief organized a twelve-man task force made up primarily of young police officers—four blacks, one Mexican and seven whites of mixed ethnic origins—and headed by a veteran who had been on the force for eighteen years. Raiding everything from bookies to prostitutes, from policy to after-hours liquor stores, the plain-clothes unit worked around the clock. It answered only to the mayor, the police chief and Assistant Police Chief Charles Boone, mainly because some of the policemen from the previous administration could not be trusted. For years the department had been plagued with corrupt officers who took bribes, stole, and served off-duty as guards for gambling dens. Yet it had been difficult to eliminate them from the force because of their civil service immunity. One case involved a police captain who actually punished an off-duty patrolman for arresting a group of gamblers. The patrolman had not been ordered to raid the gambling den. To teach him a lesson, the captain reduced him to polishing rifles. "When we found out about that," Mayor Hatcher recalls, "we just sort of blew our top."

For unorganized crime—street robberies, muggings and the like—Chief Hilton formed a special, sixteen-man tactical unit headed by Assistant Police Chief Boone and operated like the task force. In addition, the mayor proposed purchase of a police helicopter to patrol larger areas of Gary. But he was aware that the city which heretofore had taken a rather permissive attitude toward certain types of behavior was not going to reform overnight.

Indeed, in July 1968 the reform mayor disclosed that his life and that of his police chief had been threatened, apparently because of their anticrime campaign. He promptly announced: "I want to make it very clear, we are not going to abate the raids or be deterred by threats from any person, group, or organization." Nevertheless, Mayor Hatcher avoided riding in Gary's Art Festival parade during the July 13–14 weekend.

While busily fighting crime, Hatcher also became engaged in a series of crises: a school boycott and police, fire and sanitation department strikes. The school boycott had been organized in May 1968 by "The Concerned Citizens for Quality Education," a group of parents and civil rights activists who sought a clear statement from the school board supporting school integration. For several years the board had promised to develop integration guidelines. But the promises had never been fulfilled. Now the Concerned Citizens were demanding the removal of Acting Superintendent Clarence Swingley, a conservative who opposed their liberal goals.

Very early in the controversy Mayor Hatcher declared himself neutral, explaining that the city administration had no jurisdiction in the operation of the schools. However, he would be concerned as a private citizen, he added, and cited figures from a Human Relations Commission survey indicating the public schools were 83 percent segregated. These findings supported similar conclusions reached five years earlier when Mayor Hatcher was one of the lawyers in a federal suit to desegregate Gary's schools. Though they had lost the case, their research had revealed how extensively the schools were segregated. Five years had not produced even a hint of improvement. So on May 17, 1968, more than a dozen adults, led by forty-five-year-old Steve Morris, took over the Gary Public School Administration Building. Boycott of the schools by about 20,000 children was already in its fifth day. Morris' backers manned the Administration Building switchboard and turned back all incoming calls. "We are leaving at the end of the day," he promised. "We have made our point."

Meanwhile, Mayor Hatcher neither encouraged nor discouraged the boycotters. The school board had asked the mayor and all responsible citizens to take a public stand for civil obedience in the interest of the children and the entire community. But he refused to intervene until both sides asked him to bring them together to start negotiations. At first it seemed as if progress would be made. Then the board announced it would refuse to meet any further with the boycotters.

Into the limelight stepped an all-white group, "Citizens to Save Our Schools," announcing they were going to visit the mayor. They were welcome to come, just like anyone else, he said. So they came to complain that they were sick of people like Steve Morris attempting to take over their schools. Mayor Hatcher promised to enforce the law no matter who it applied to. He recalls:

> *Then they went back and announced to the press that the following morning they were going to march 1,000 strong down to City Hall. I told a reporter they were welcome to come. I would be happy to talk to them as long as they stayed within the bounds of the law. They postponed it the next day to the following day to have more people on hand. I really was not concerned about that and was still willing to meet with them. Then we received this intelli-*

gence out of the black community that there was a group that was organizing and they were going to come down with guns and knives and interpose themselves between us and these people. They were not going to permit them to come down. What we were going to have on our hands could very well be a bloody mess. It was at that point that I felt both sides had reached the point where it was going to be a physical kind of fight and the well-being of the city was in jeopardy. At that point I had to step in and in effect call the boycott off. I phoned Steve Morris and explained the situation to him and asked him to call it off. He did.

Morris, who had been a $5,700-a-year school lunch program clerk in a township trustee's office, was later hired as a $10,500-a-year "senior coordinator" in the Concentrated Employment Program. The school board complied with all of the boycotters' demands, getting rid of the superintendent, issuing a policy statement supporting integration and drawing new boundaries for a West Side high school under construction. In the process, Gary also secured as its new schools superintendent, forty-two-year-old Gordon McAndrews, reputed to be one of the nation's six best superintendents. Long before coming to his $30,000-a-year post he had made a reputation integrating schools in North Carolina. Now he promised to build on the "confrontation between white and black" to make Gary's schools among the nation's best.

That confrontation had hardly been resolved when another occurred in the police department. With starting salaries scaled at $7,020, policemen asked for a $1,000-a-year raise. Mayor Hatcher had indicated to all city departments that in the first year of his administration he was adopting an austerity program. There would be no pay increases except in very selective cases. Gary's tax base was seriously eroded and he was anxious to tear down slum housing that was not producing tax revenue and replace it with tax-producing, new housing. The Mayor explained that by the second year of his administration it would be in position to ask for substantial increases for city employes.

He had told Police Chief Hilton, in particular, that policemen should not ask for substantial raises. The mayor wanted to develop more control within the department, because it was still laced with corrupt policemen. Giving a corrupt policeman a $1,000 raise, he felt, amounted to rewarding a crook.

But the policemen carried their case to the Gary City Council with arguments showing how much they were worth to the community and how little return they were receiving for their efforts. In the midst of the negotiations some sixty policemen, with the so-called blue flu, phoned in sick on an eight-to-four morning shift. Mayor Hatcher had known a day earlier that the informal strike was coming and had gone to court and secured a temporary restraining order which was served on every member of the police department. By the start of the evening shift at four, all were back to work. Within hours, however, the City Council granted them a flat raise of $1,000 for 1969. Gary's firemen sought but failed to receive a similar salary increase. A later strike of garbage collectors ended after two days when the Gary City Council approved a $39,000 money bill to restore the five-day work week which had been cut back to four days.

Gary escaped two other possible crises in 1968. Following the April 4 assassination of Dr. Martin Luther King rioting erupted in 125 U.S. cities. At least forty-six persons were killed, all but five of whom were blacks. More than 3,500 persons were injured, more than $45 million worth of propetry was lost by fire or looting and more than 20,000 arrests were made. But the tornado passed over Gary. It could have hit there, when two hundred black high school students stormed out of classes. But Mayor Hatcher met them before they had gone two blocks and persuaded them to return to their studies.

In July, however, violence erupted early one Sunday morning when several Gary citizens were wounded by apparently indiscriminate gun fire. One of them, a Gary fireman, was hit while performing his duties and required hospitalization. The outburst of lawlessness, during which three stores were set afire, was contained within two hours. The next night, however, there were some close calls although the end results were only broken windows and a damaged street light. Gary had not had a full-scale riot. The 550 National Guardsmen who were alerted remained outside the city at Mayor Hatcher's request. Looting, though evident, had not been conducted on a wholesale basis. Some 127 arrests had been made. It was clear that the city had not been made immune to violence and civil disorder by the election of a black mayor.

Mayor Hatcher himself was not immune to attacks from his own, heavily black City Council. For many reasons—"political, lack of vision, lack of understanding"—the Council, in his view, was an obstacle to many of the programs he was trying to launch. Four of the nine councilmen elected in the November 1967 election had been black, but two of them were holdovers from the Katz machine and thus opposed Hatcher almost reflexively. A third, Muigwithania member Dozier Allen, also clashed with the Mayor. Of the five white councilmen, three consistently voted against Hatcher. Many of the councilmen openly complained about not receiving their "fair share of jobs," referring to the demise of the old patronage system under which jobs and sums of money were funneled through the City Council. Thus, for example, corrupt councilmen in previous administrations reportedly were paid $1,700 for firemen's jobs and a smaller sum for positions in the police department. Firemen paid the larger sum, because their work schedules were such that they could "moonlight" and thus reap two incomes.

The communications breakdown between the Mayor and his inherently hostile Council has been one of the major failures of his regime, despite his early attempts at free and easy dialogue through bi-weekly meetings of the councilmen at his home. Councilmen, even those sympathetic to the mayor, complained that they found it difficult to obtain information from him and claimed his department heads only spoke in generalities. Part of the problem they attributed to the mayor's unwillingness to delegate authority to subordinates, a charge also made by former Corporation Counsel Hilbert Bradley and others. "A cut was made in the mayor's personnel budget," Council President Quentin P. Smith informed a newsman. "The next day in the paper I see that because of my actions the city has lost $350,000 in Federal funds. I tell the mayor: 'Your man was here yesterday and he didn't say anything to warn me.' Brother, that's a communication gap!"

During his first year in office, Mayor Hatcher was attacked by several councilmen for what they termed unnecessary absences from the city, leaving city problems unattended. One councilman, Democrat Paul Dudak, claimed the mayor's absences would result in a breakdown in local government. Another, Democrat Dozier Allen, charged that Hatcher had been disrespectful to the Council while a third member, Republican Eugene M. Kirkland, sarcastically suggested that someone should give the mayor a list of the Council members so that he would know who they were. Kirkland claimed at one point that he had sought audiences with Hatcher on six different occasions but had seen him only once. To the absentee charge, Mayor Hatcher replies:

I'm not an absentee mayor. I probably spend more time working at the job of being mayor than perhaps any other mayor in the city's history. I work seven days a week. Saturday and Sunday are just like every other day. The only time I'm not working on city business is when I just make myself take a couple hours off. People who are close to me are always telling me that I really ought to take more time away from the duties of the office. But I know there's a great deal that has to be done.

When I ran for the office, I understood it was not a nine-to-five job and I've been willing to make that kind of effort. The criticism is always as if my going out of town represents some kind of vacation when it's just the contrary. Most of the time—even on a speaking engagement for instance—I meet with city officials of that city. We discuss some of the things they're doing, some of the problems they're having. We exchange ideas. The idea of the storefront police station we have came from a trip to Baltimore where I was to make a speech. I met with the mayor and he was telling me he had this new idea of a storefront police station, and that it was working well. He took me down to look at one. I returned to Gary and we got the ball rolling and today Gary has a storefront police station.

I don't apologize for being out of town. I'm very happy that people are not criticizing me for stealing money. I would rather they criticize me by saying, "Well he goes out of town a lot." I've talked to many mayors and they all tell me they get the same criticism.

Much of the criticism of Mayor Hatcher during the early days of his administration came from the *Gary Post-Tribune* which opposed his candidacy. "In certain areas he's done a very good job," admitted Managing Editor James Rasmusen. "I can't be anything but complimentary on his handling of touchy situations in Gary. He did a good job in keeping the city cool after the assassination of Martin Luther King. He and the police chief and members of the Indiana state championship basketball team were out on the streets keeping the calm then, and again at a big fire at a lumber company [during the firemen's strike] when he got the crowd to disperse." Rasmusen listed "federal assistance for people who are potentially a problem," and recreation and job programs as other positive accomplishments. Then he defended his paper against Hatcher's charge that it had had "a fairly negative approach." The Mayor argues:

> *The newspaper has tended to emphasize the negative and deemphasize the positive so that one has to go outside of Gary to get the positive picture of what is taking place here. The Chicago, Washington and New York newspapers on the whole have printed positive stories about Gary. But the local paper emphasizes things like my failure to be at a meeting on time, not mentioning the fact that I'm probably the busiest mayor that Gary has ever had. There are greater demands on my time than perhaps any mayor that Gary has had before. But they'll say that the mayor was ten minutes late coming to, say, a press conference. It doesn't matter that at that same press conference I might have announced a multi-million-*

dollar program for Gary. They downplay that and emphasize the fact that I was late. They don't mention the fact that previous mayors never had press conferences. That's the problem. Many of the good things that are happening, the city people don't know about them unless they are personally involved, because the newspaper does not tell the overall story.

Critics other than the *Gary Post-Tribune*, during Mayor Hatcher's first year in office, accused him of being "bigheaded," a "dictator" and more concerned about his public image than Gary. They charged he turned over to federal experts too much of the responsibility for plotting Gary's future and kept to himself too much of the responsibility for day-to-day management of the city—even to the point of hiring secretaries for city departments. "The joke around the mayor's office is that he climbed to the top and pulled the ladder up behind him," lamented a black businessman who worked in Hatcher's campaign. And the heavily critical Councilman Dozier Allen complained:

> *Not too long ago I was interviewed on one of the local radio stations, on a program called "Sound-Off" where the listening audience can call in and ask questions. One of the callers said to me, "Mr. Allen, I don't think you should be critical of the Mayor, because you know and I know and everyone else knows Mayor Hatcher is a God-sent man." I didn't respond, but I felt like saying, "So was Moses and David—God-sent men. But somewhere along the line each man deviated from the favor of God."*

Whether for divine or other reasons, Mayor Hatcher, dur-

ing the first year of his administration, was accused of being
a weak administrator. Critics said he did not keep his own
schedules, that he had to be pushed and nudged to keep appointments, that he tended to operate in a fashion too free-
wheeling for a city already plagued with administrative chaos.
Again and again critics charged him with being too attentive
to trivial detail. "He doesn't like a situation where someone
who is working for him knows more about a particular thing
than he does, which I think is a kind of insecurity," declared
one administrator. "You're supposed to want your staff to
know more about a situation than you do. But not him."

Good administrator? Poor administrator? The deposed Hilbert Bradley analyzed the problem this way:

> *One can be like Ike Eisenhower and select good
> departmental heads, delegate the authority to these
> and then go out and shoot some golf. That's one type
> of administrator and he is still a good administrator.
> Or you can be like John F. Kennedy, the kind of
> man who was articulate, remained on the local scene
> and requested all kinds of information to be fur-
> nished by departmental heads who remained in
> Washington and supervised most of the projects. My
> contention is that you can be one or the other of
> these types of administrators, but you cannot be
> both. I think Hatcher has a tendency to feel that he
> can be both. He makes speeches all over the nation,
> which is good. He's been down to Washington for
> all kinds of programs which is also wonderful. But
> he has to be like Eisenhower and delegate authority
> or like John Kennedy and remain on the scene daily.*

The accuracy of Bradley's analysis, the validity of other
criticisms of Mayor Hatcher depends in the final analysis on

whether in fact he successfully grappled with the problems that confronted Gary. Much of the criticism during his first year was premature. Much of it also arose out of conscious and unconscious comparisons of Gary with such advanced and sophisticated municipalities as Chicago, New York, and Los Angeles. Because he became a national celebrity of sorts overnight, Mayor Hatcher was expected to produce at an extraordinarily high and unrealistic level. The extent to which he was able to rise to these expectations remained to be seen.

6. Trials and Triumphs

6. Trials and Triumphs

THE RUNNING BATTLE between Mayor Hatcher and the Gary City Council moved on into 1969 and continued to bedevil his administration. Early in the year councilman-at-large John Armenta, a Mexican allied with Gary's political old guard, introduced a proposal which would have reduced the mayor's power to appoint members to the Human Relations Commission. Instead of selecting all fifteen commissioners, he would be empowered to name only six. Then each of the nine councilmen would appoint one each.

This same sort of issue—who should appoint Commission members?—had been thoroughly debated when Hatcher himself served on the Gary City Council. Some of his colleagues argued that appointments by councilmen could be misused to pay off political debts. On the other hand, if the mayor did the appointing, then the Council could vote his choices up or down and thus force him to select qualified persons rather than political hacks.

As reasonable as this arrangement may have seemed, it was unsatisfactory to Armenta. Not only that, his colleagues unanimously approved the first and second reading of his proposed bill. Its passage was going to be a cinch. That is, if Mayor Hatcher lay dead. But his political instincts told him he had to act. Just before the bill was to receive final consideration by the City Council, he instructed several of his department heads to attend the crucial session and speak against the proposed law. They were not the only concerned parties who showed up, however, on the evening when the councilmen—three whites, the Mexican and five blacks—gathered to deliberate. They were greeted by a cross-section of the black community—Ph.D.'s and NoD.'s, precinct officials and members of the League of Voters, NAACPers, and more than two hundred members of Gary's youth gangs who probably had never before attended a City Council session. No matter. Their hero was on trial. Most were convinced that the issue before them was a naked power play by the Council to strip Mayor Hatcher of some of his appointive powers.

"A lot of us didn't know at first why we came down here," declared Ronald Bryant, vice-president of the Kangaroos, speaking into a floor microphone. "But now we know!"

Kenneth (Sunny) McGee, president of the Sin City Disciples, warned the Council that anytime the Mayor needed his (McGee's) gang, he only had to "pull our leash and we bark and we bark hard." The Council chambers rang with cheers accented by Black Power salutes.

Then there was a stillness as a glowering black youth in African regalia faced the assembly and announced his name as Elemi Olorumfummi. "When that cat stood up in that daishiki and gave them that Olorumfummi business," a Hatcher aide later remarked, "man, their minds were all messed up from then on."

Olorumfummi demanded: "What you want us to have? Nothing? You crawin' with us. And we tired. Tired of playin'. The game is over. We make this clear, this is not a threat. This is a promise."

Another African-garbed spokesman stepped to the microphone, identified himself as Henry Gill, then told the Council: "If you're gonna take this thing and checkmate it and play a chess game with it, then you'd better think twice. Today, tonight, please, for God's sake let it be heard here, let it be heard through the country that we're gonna back Mayor Hatcher from hell to eternity." Another explosion of whoops and applause was briskly gaveled down by Council President Quinton Smith.

A school teacher rose to say Mayor Hatcher had done more for Gary in a short time than any other mayor, then added: "Your effort to attack my mayor is going to hasten your slide into Hell. I want you to know that sliding in is going to be a lot easier than getting out. I want you to know we're supporting Mayor Hatcher 100 percent as long as he's mayor and as long as he's black."

By now thoroughly aroused by the angry testimonials, Councilman Paul Dudak called for a fifteen-minute recess and proposed that the Council meet in an executive session with the mayor. But Hatcher declined, explaining: "I'm not interested in sitting in a closed-door meeting with the Council. What I have to say, I will say here where everyone can hear."

The Council recessed behind closed doors without Hatcher. When they returned, Dudak beckoned three newsmen over to where the Mayor was seated and said excitedly: "Now I'm asking him in front of you fellows! I'm asking for police protection!"

"Mr. Dudak, if you want police protection, we will give it to you," Hatcher promised.

But Dudak was not satisfied. He began speaking to the Council and charging that Hatcher had been responsible for what he felt was a threatening situation. Then just as he was claiming that no policemen were in the packed chamber, two giant black patrolmen slipped in behind him. The councilman became so confused he lapsed into a long speech about how much he had supported the mayor's programs in the Council. "I might have made speeches against him," he

claimed, "but when the vote came I always voted with him."
Had he? According to Hatcher, the councilman had in fact
never backed him at all.

As the time came to vote on the motion, Councilman
Eugene Kirkland claimed: "I'll have to confess, sitting here
tonight at this performance, that I'm in no mental condition
to vote intelligently on legislation. . . . We are anxious and
glad to hear personal opinion, but when he hear personal attack and threats of personal violence, under these conditions
. . . frankly, I'm in no condition to vote on this myself mentally tonight either way." Thus he abstained, while two other
councilmen (Armenta and Dudak) voted for the motion and
six voted against it. With the bill defeated after two and a
half hours of stormy debate, Mayor Hatcher left the Council
chambers.

But the issue was far from settled. Too many wounds had
been inflicted. Press and radio commentators charged the next
day that Hatcher should have warned the youth gang leaders
that their kind of behavior was not acceptable. The fact that
they had not actually violated any of the City Council's rules
did not matter. Some critics openly accused Mayor Hatcher
of being responsible for the attendance of the youths, while
an editorial writer dubbed the whole affair as "gunboat diplo-
macy," an effort to "legislate by fear." News stories quoted
the youth leaders at length and then, as if they were footnotes,
tacked on brief mentions of the equally vocal opposition to
Armenta's bill from the Urban League, NAACP, League of
Women Voters, and other "respectable" organizations. Mayor
Hatcher recalls:

> *The next morning my whole press conference was*
> *taken up with questions about the deliberations.*
> *The reporters were so shaken they were angry. They*
> *were ready to take me apart. They said that two of*

the councilmen had threatened to resign. I asked what two. The two were Eugene Kirkland and Dozier Allen. A reporter told me he would have ordered every one of them (the youth gang members) out of the Council Chambers, because their presence intimidated people. And that was the mood of the newspapers generally. But I visited a number of taverns and other public places that night and it was interesting what that City Council session had done for the black community. Everywhere I went people were introducing me as their hero and saying I had stood up to my opponents. It was a beautiful thing, the sort of thing you dream about—that one day black people are going to be united and say we know who the enemy is. We now have some very enlightened councilmen. They are not going to go down there any more and just vote black people down the river without even thinking about it twice. They will never be the same again.

Gary, too, had changed. Pressure rather than parliamentary politics was the order of the day. Shortly after the momentous City Council session, some 150 demonstrators—about half of them women and children—ambushed a Republican fundraising dinner at the Gary armory for Indiana Governor Edgar D. Whitcomb, who had resolutely ignored their appeals to discuss proposed welfare legislation. The affair had been purposely scheduled at the armory, in the heart of the black community, to attract more blacks to the Republican party.

Instead it attracted angry demonstrators who included disgruntled school teachers, mental health employees and students from Indiana University. Leading the group was the Aid for Dependent Children (AFDC) Mothers Club which had sent representatives to Indianapolis months earlier to testify before a legislative committee considering a welfare-reform bill. Their complaint was that the State of Indiana provided only 40 percent of the funds needed to properly feed and clothe a family. Thus, for example, a mother of two received only ninety-seven dollars a month and if she became employed her welfare allotment was terminated. The welfare mothers argued that welfare programs in Indiana's bordering states, Ohio, Michigan, and Illinois, were far more liberal and more in line with the prevailing cost of living.

The welfare reform bill sought by the AFDC Mothers passed both houses of the Indiana legislature and was sent to Governor Whitcomb for signature. The bill had overcome two obstacles, but, as far as the welfare mothers were concerned, there was no guarantee it would survive the third. Their representatives returned to Indianapolis to ask the governor not to veto the bill, which called for an increase in welfare allotments. He gave them less than two minutes of his time. He was going to do "what was right," he promised ambiguously. He vetoed the bill.

But the AFDC Mothers had not given up their fight. Turning to Mayor Hatcher, they asked him to intercede with Governor Whitcomb on their behalf. And the mayor obligingly wired the governor requesting that when he attended the fund-raising dinner in Gary he or one of his representatives meet with the AFDC mothers. Since the governor made no reply to the wire, one of Hatcher's aides phoned his office the day before he was due in Gary and was told that Governor Whitcomb had the telegram "in his pocket." Furthermore, he was not going to make a decision on the proposed meeting until after his Gary arrival.

Such indecision was enough for the AFDC mothers to organize a march on the Gary Armory of about 150 demonstrators—40 percent of them children under ten years of age or women. Arriving in a cold rain, the small army at first camped at the side of the building, then invaded the premises.

Once inside, they began singing and marching around tables already set up for the fund-raising dinner and some of the children sat down and began eating pie that had been brought out. Asked the reason for the "eat in," their mothers replied angrily: "The children are hungry." Meanwhile, Mayor Hatcher was at home getting himself together to introduce Governor Whitcomb at the dinner as a matter of courtesy to Indiana's highest elected official. When police phoned and informed him of events at the Armory, he spoke to the AFDC spokesman, Mrs. Zola Tomlin, and persuaded her to clear demonstrators from the building. Hatcher arrived later and learned the demonstrators who were now outside the Armory still wanted to meet with the governor. He recalls:

> *About an hour later when Governor Whitcomb's aides finally decided to let me speak with him, I asked "What do you intend to do? Are you coming? I can't get anybody to make a decision about whether they want to go on with the dinner or not." He came up with something like it was not up to them to make a decision; "It's up to your police department to provide protection." I said: "Governor, if you intend to come, the demonstrators would like to meet with you or a representative to talk about a special legislative session." He said: "I came up here to make a speech. I didn't come up here to meet with anybody." I said: "Fine! I'll go down and clear the way so you can come and make your speech." I told the demonstrators what he said and that he was not coming to make his speech until everything was all cleared away. I told them I would keep working to try to bring about a meeting for them with the gov-*

*ernor, but I could not make any promises. I asked
them: "In my best interest, will you leave? At this
point, there is not much more to be gained." Just
like that they left. They didn't want to do anything
to embarrass me. The governor came down and made
his speech. He said something like: "I wish those
people had been here so I could tell them what all
we are doing for them in the State of Indiana."*

The next day Indiana's attorney general Theodore Sendak,
who had not witnessed the Armory events, declared they con-
firmed "a reign of terror" was loose in Gary. And in a brief
spasm of bipartisanship, John Krupa, chairman of the Lake
County Democratic organization, volunteered that what the
affront to the Republican governor meant was Gary could
use a spell as a "police state."

At the next City Council meeting, one Republican member described the events, somewhat ambitiously, as "a new day
of infamy" which had destroyed "our image through the
United States, and the world." Hatcher insisted, "Somehow,
children eating pie do not call up an image of terror." Later,
in private, he argued: "Most of that noise is coming from the
bigots, and I'm not going to occupy myself forever pacifying
them. Anyway, they wouldn't be pacified if I walked down
Broadway [Gary's main street] on my hands."

Meanwhile, Governor Whitcomb, responding to pressure
from his party, backed Sendak by saying Garyites "need outside help" and by announcing that State Police were con-
ducting an investigation. Hatcher lashed back at the two
Republicans, charging that the reign-of-terror statement was
reckless, irresponsible, and false. Again, he recalls:

About three or four days later the governor called

my office while I was in New York and asked if I would please come down to a luncheon that he was holding the next day in Indianapolis. When I got there it was very obvious that he was trying to smooth over the troubled waters because he had me sitting right at his right elbow. He had other mayors from around the state, but had me at this special, reserved place. He made reference to the fine job Mayor Hatcher was doing in Gary and claimed he wanted to help me with more housing and so forth. Then we had a serious private conversation and I said: "Governor, those statements by Sendak certainly didn't help us at all." He said: "I know, but after all we're new. You're new and I'm new and we're both sort of feeling our way around. I think the best thing for both of us to do is not look back. Just look forward. We're not going to let that interrupt our own relationship and all the things you have been trying to do in Gary." I said: "That's true, but I think it's going to take some kind of statement in view of the other statement, some kind of counterstatement to correct the false impression that has been given." I left, but later on that afternoon he insisted that I ride in his limousine with him. When I got back home someone asked me: "Did you know the governor called another press conference. Sounds like he's trying to kiss and make up. He came out with the statement that there were no differences between you and him and you were doing a fine job in Gary."

The tragic part about the whole business is that in all of the furor about a few pieces of pie, the real issues got lost and they are still there. The welfare

*reform bill that Governor Whitcomb vetoed, be-
cause of insufficient funds, would have improved the
welfare situation.*

Slingshots from the City Council, barbed arrows from the
Republican Party, these, were child's play in comparison with
Mayor Hatcher's basic struggle to keep Gary from disinte-
grating altogether. The catalyst for that disintegration was
Glen Park—a quiet, tidy community of neat brick bungalows
and manicured lawns. It was this superficially peaceful sub-
urb where petitions were circulated in 1969 calling for its
secession from the city. The move was promoted more or
less overtly by the area's councilman, Eugene Kirkland, a
fiftyish, chunky, bespectacled real estate broker. Much of the
secession leadership also came from steelworker Robert K.
Stephenson who told a national magazine: "As far as we're
concerned, Gary is dead. The citizens of Glen Park feel they
don't benefit from being part of the city of Gary. We have no
say in what the city does with our tax money and we feel it's
time we had control of our own destiny."

So Stephenson and a group of thirty friends launched a
dead-serious effort to split Gary in two, "disannexing" Glen
Park and its 42,000 citizens from the city. Their ambitious
program was going to require at least three stages. First they
would have to collect signatures from 51 percent of Glen
Park's property owners. Then they would have to submit the
petition to the Gary Board of Works, which would be sure
to shove it right back at them since its three members were
appointed by Hatcher. Finally, they could drag the issue
through the courts for months. If they were successful, then
disannexation would be a fact.

The community was already physically divided from the
grimy steel town by the rancid Calumet River, a flowing sump
for the industrial wastes of the steel mills. The cultural gap

was even wider, since Glen Park is a stronghold of blue-collar aristocrats—foremen and skilled workers with settled, conservative ways—while the rest of Gary teems with restless, unskilled and often unemployed men. And to cap the divisive situation, there are only forty black families in all of Glen Park. In the rest of Gary, three-quarters of the 138,000 residents are black.

Talk of secession had been endemic in Glen Park for years, then gained ground in 1967 with the election of Gary's first black mayor. But it was not until the summer of 1969, when Hatcher announced plans to build up a low-cost, welfare housing project in Glen Park, that the movement began to flower.

"People were afraid that the project would draw not only Negroes, but the worst type of Negroes," Councilman Kirkland explained. A few Glen Parkers chipped in to hire an attorney to fight the project, but soon ran out of money. Then Stephenson, the Republican precinct captain, started talking up secession and received some support from his Democratic counterpart, Rudy Bartolomie. Ostensibly, the complaints were economic. Glen Park residents argued they did not get a tax dollar's worth of public services. But as Stephenson saw it, this too was a racial problem. "If we had a white mayor," he lamented, "we would have more response to our problems and complaints."

But had not Hatcher sworn to be mayor of all the people? He fought now to preserve his city and the solid tax base furnished by Glen Park's average family income of about $12,000. A Glen Park Information Committee had organized to oppose disannexation and invited Hatcher to present the case against it in a series of house meetings. In one of those meetings with a group of Glen Park residents he warned that if their section disannexed from Gary, it would show the world that democracy had not worked. Whatever problems existed in the city, he argued, could be solved by everyone working together.

Prepared for the possibility that this sort of appeal might not impress his listeners, Hatcher had brought with him his special assistant on finances, Glen Vantrease, who detailed some of the financial problems that would come with disannexation. Glen Park would have an assessed valuation of $30 to $40 million which would be insufficient to operate a separate government, he pointed out. Under state law, Glen Park would have to have a mayor, a police chief, nine city councilmen, a city attorney, a city judge and a comptroller. It would have to provide its own city court, police station, city jail, police cars, police and firemen, clerical staff, etc.

Vantrease noted that "the present per capita assessed valuation in Gary [was] $1,829 (dividing the city's total evaluation by its population)." After subtracting the value of the steelworks to the north, the per capita assessed valuation of Glen Park would drop to less than $850. "This would be the lowest per capita assessed valuation in the State of Indiana," he argued.

Then too, since disannexation did not carry an automatic secession from other taxing units, Glen Park would find itself with other governing boards that were not appointed from its own community—particularly schools, library, and sanitary districts. Vantrease also pointed out that Glen Park would have to acquire its own garbage trucks or contract with a private scavenger to haul refuse and probably would have to operate its own city dump.

On the other hand, what were some of the advantages that Glen Park received as part of Gary? Vantrease pointed out that hundreds of thousands of dollars had been spent the previous year for garbage removal, maintenance of the city dump, snow removal, street repairs and street sweeping, maintenance of two golf courses, the baseball stadium and other recreational facilities. In other words, in 1968 Glen Park had received $193,000 worth of police protection, $368,000 in fire protection, twenty school crossing guards at $34,000, some $13,500 worth of electricity to operate traffic signals, another $87,200 for street lights and $12,500 for fire hydrants. All of these services for Glen Park totalled nearly $750,000.

For those listeners still unconvinced of the folly of disannexation, Gary's Model Cities director, William Staehle, pointed out that a lopped off Glen Park would not be eligible for federal money for such projects as the revamping of its decrepit sewage system. And since the project would cost about $50 million, it was unlikely it could be completed in the immediate future without government funds. The cumulative weight of these arguments crushed most of the secession sentiment and Glen Park settled down quieter than a mouse.

But a lion roared in the Gary City Council. Dozier Allen, who had teamed with Hatcher and others in the founding of Muigwithania and then differed with him over 1967 election campaign strategy, now challenged him to a public debate on his handling of street gangs and street violence in the city. He had first criticized the mayor's handling of the gangs after the explosive City Council meeting when several gang members using colorful language successfully protested Councilman Armenta's bill to strip Hatcher of some of his appointive power.

Councilman Allen prefaced his newest challenge with the claim that he was not running for mayor, then argued that twenty separate gangs were active in the city with at least one claiming more than one thousand members. He charged that gang members had gained enough influence with Gary's police chief to be issued courtesy cards which amounted to a handcuff on junior police officers. Allen said there was a familiar saying in the city that people would rather have the police " 'catch me with my gun than the hoodlums catch me without it.' This extremely dangerous point has been reached in Gary due to the attitude of Gary's mayor." This was not to say Hatcher bore all the blame. Some of it had to be shared by the City Council, the Human Relations Commission and influential members of the public. But Allen insisted the greatest fault lay with the Mayor because he had more legal power than any single person in the city. The councilman called for a hard line policy against gang members, because in his view the escalation of gang activity was slowly choking Gary's black community to death. This, then, was the substance of his proposed debate with Mayor Hatcher.

"What we need at this point is not debate but action," Hatcher replied. Later Allen accused him of deliberately "coddling" gangs to put together "a unit for political activity in the future . . . to harass and intimidate political rallies and individual supporters [of anti-Hatcher candidates]." The councilman also charged the mayor had included street gang chieftains in political strategy sessions. "That's absolutely false," was Hatcher's only comment.

During the first two years of his administration he had learned to live with these and other sensational charges. They had not deterred his efforts to deal effectively with the problems that confronted Gary. In his February 1970 "State of the City" address, he delivered what amounted to "a report to the stockholders on the status of the muni-corporation of Gary." The metaphor contemplated each citizen as a shareholder in Gary's present and future and Hatcher was reporting as a "company man" committed to the realization of Gary's promise.

The mayor's prospectus of Gary singled out a scarcity of money as one of the city's prominent problems. That is, "an increased demand for services from government continually [smashed] headlong into an inadequate tax base." Gary still depended on a property tax for 80 percent of its municipal income and desperately needed to find alternative sources of income. About $35 million had come into the city during the past two years from federal sources for education, manpower programs, urban renewal, code enforcement, neighborhood facilities, poverty programs, law enforcement, health, and beautification.

Yet the federal money had not kept Gary's crime rate from rising by about 4 percent (or well below the national average increase) in 1969. On the other hand, a partnership between the city government, the federal government and the private sector had yielded a total of 2,089 new housing units. "The benefits of this sharp upswing are far-reaching," Mayor Hatcher reported. "First there are the 2,089 families, that is, more than 9,000 people, who live in better homes than they did two years ago. In addition . . . some $35 million in fresh money has been introduced to Gary's economy. Of that impressive sum, more than $17 million is being spent on housing materials, with the major portion purchased from Gary merchants and suppliers. More than one thousand man-years of work for construction tradesmen has been provided by this sudden and steep housing climb. This is equivalent to one thousand year-round jobs and represents total wages of $8.5 million."

Two years earlier, Gary had been plagued with 20,400 housing units that needed minor repairs; 7,400 units so unsound they required replacement; 13,800 units that needed major repair and an almost non-existent local code enforcement program. Now Mayor Hatcher could report that his Building Department had upped its inspections from considerably less than six thousand to more than fifty thousand per year. More than five hundred substandard units had been brought into line with code standards and the mayor had applied for a federally assisted concentrated code enforcement program to bring three housand more units up to code specifications.

Hatcher also hoped for aid from President Nixon's new National Air and Water Pollution Control Program to help deal with Gary's air pollution. Through the Air Pollution Control Division of the Board of Health, the quality of Gary air had improved by 34 percent in 1969.

In the area of education, Mayor Hatcher reported that underfinancing had led to the curtailment of educational programs and a threat to close the schools. On the other hand, there had also been measurable progress. Money had been garnered for pre-school programs, for deprived children, the emotionally disturbed, multiply handicapped and mentally retarded kids. Money had also come for library and educational materials for Title I schools in poverty areas—and nine thousand poor youngsters had been direct beneficiaries. Para-professionals had been trained to assist in the classroom, and programs had been generated to provide college opportunities to disadvantaged young people. And there was the future possibility of increased funding from the federal government for special education, and for increased state funding to meet the local financial crisis.

Near the end of his long "State of the City" address, Mayor Hatcher announced formation of an open-ended "Goals for Gary" Commission, composed of community leaders, young people, old people, white people, brown people, black people, from every section of Gary and from all political and religious persuasions. He recommended that the Commission form committees to conduct public hearings on every major area of need in the community, and involving every part of Gary. The Commission would begin to define the concerns of Gary's citizens as the citizens saw them, set priorities, devise programs and plans to meet those concerns and seek out ways to make possible the implementation of those programs and plans. Mayor Hatcher saw the Commission's work as supplementing rather than supplanting already existing efforts to improve Gary. Then he spoke as if he saw his future intertwined with Gary's for years to come:

We can soar in this city, if once we set our wills of steel to the chore ahead. It won't be easy; but we can soar. And in so doing, we can show the way to a generation.

That possibility is real, and it is a possibility so exciting that I can't think of another city anyone would want to live in and participate in during these critical times.

Gary can make an important difference in the crucial American seventies. Each of us can make a crucial difference in Gary.

Let's get on with the job. Together.

Epilogue

Epilogue

DURING THE 1970s any number of American cities will approximate the racial balance of Gary. Given that prospect, the question posed for black people is: How can they take political control of these cities and thus have a voice in determining the terms of their existence? Political control implies political action. When black people got together and fought for control of the schools in their community, that was political action. When they exploded in the streets, pushed beyond endurance by racist cops, gouging merchants and landlords and all the other miseries of ghetto life, that too was a kind of politics.

The trouble with these attempts to change the policies that affect the black community is that they were limited, sporadic, unorganized, semi-conscious and unsustained. It is clear now that such mass action would have been far more effective had it been combined with an organized struggle to gain political power. Such a struggle—undramatic, unpublicized but culminating in the election of Mayor Richard G. Hatcher—has been going on in Gary since the late 1950s when the reform-minded Muigwithania was founded. The question now is whether blacks in other cities will follow and improve upon Gary's example.

One answer comes out of Newark, N.J., where in June 1970 a 38-year-old engineer, Kenneth L. Gibson, defeated incumbent Mayor Hugh Addonizio 54,892 votes to 43,339 in a run-off election. Gibson had led Addonizio by a ratio of two-to-one in the six-man primary a month earlier, but was forced into the runoff when he failed to get a majority. Although Blacks and Puerto Ricans constitute 63 percent of Newark's 403,000 residents, white voters were still in the majority. Black candidates in the primary received 45 percent of the total vote while whites polled 55 percent. In the runoff, Gibson received substantial white backing partially because Addonizio was under federal indictment on charges of tax evasion, conspiracy and extortion, and partially because the incumbent had waged a vicious campaign of racial smears.

Meanwhile, movements toward black political empowerment are well underway in Cleveland; Detroit; Los Angeles; Atlanta; Buffalo; New York; Hartford and Waterbury, Connecticut; Dayton, Ohio, and a few other cities. Blacks vied for the mayorship in these cities during the 1969 elections. Backed by almost all of Cleveland's 38-percent black population, Mayor Carl B. Stokes won a close battle for reelection. But Richard H. Austin, a black Democrat running for mayor in Detroit, lost by a narrow margin to Republican Wayne County Sheriff Roman S. Gribbs. A one-time bootblack who rose to county auditor, Austin was the first black ever to seek the mayorship of the city that witnessed the worst riots in the nation's history only two years earlier. Most of Detroit's 30 percent black population voted in a bloc for Austin, while an overwhelming majority of white votes went for Gribbs.

In Buffalo, where the "law and order" theme was voiced most throughout the 1969 elections, black independent Ambrose I. Lane ran a poor third, partially because incumbent Democrat Frank A. Sedita did well in the city's black areas. The same was true in Hartford where the first black mayoral candidate in the city's 334-year history, NAACP official Wil-

bur Smith, finished third to incumbent Mayor Ann Uccello
—the only woman mayor of a state capital.

Meanwhile, Boswell Trowers, a black civil rights activist
running on the "Citizens for Progress" ticket in Waterbury,
polled only 937 votes and finished a poor fourth. And in
Dayton, millionaire Dave Hall won by a two-to-one margin
despite efforts by the city's black community to elect Lawrence Nelson, a black foundry worker.

In most of these cities the black candidates were as qualified for the mayor's office as were the white incumbents. But
in too many cases, black voters did not see fit to support
them. Many still voted for the white office-seeker, who they
felt was what Hawkins calls the "least evil" of the candidates,
and then watched in dismay as he turned his back on them
once he was elected.[1]

But Gary's black voters cast their lot with a man whose
public career as a civil rights activist had already shown him
to be committed to the liberation of black people from inadequate housing, mediocre schools, inferior health facilities, and
economic and political powerlessness. What is especially important about Mayor Hatcher's election is that it demonstrated
that an independent could buck the entrenched political machine and win. He was not saddled with the near-impossible
task of reforming the racist Democratic or Republican parties
in that city. Nor did he undertake the equally formidable job
of organizing an all-black party. In short, he made the most
of a monstrously bad situation.

This was because Hatcher's political style is essentially reformist rather than revolutionary. Instead of trying to destroy
"the system"—a probable impossibility for him or anyone
else at this time—he is doing the next best thing. He is working diligently within it to bring about change. As economist

1. Reginald Hawkins, "I Still Exist," *The Black Politician*, vol. 1, no. 3 (January,
1970), p. 21.

Robert S. Browne, cited in the foreword of this book, says, the mayor sees the political process as only one of many tactics black people must use to bring about their liberation. He points out that other ethnic groups, through political action, have carved a slice of the political and economic pie for themselves. Yet Hatcher has no illusions about the extent of his power in Gary. "There is much talk about black control of the ghetto," he has said. "What does it mean? I am mayor of a city of roughly ninety thousand black people—but we do not control the possibilities of jobs for them, of money for their schools, or state-funded social institutions. These things are in the hands of U.S. Steel Corporation, the county department of welfare, and the State of Indiana."

In other words, Hatcher understands that total black control of schools, jobs, cities, or anything else in this racist country is now and will probably always be an illusion. At best, blacks have what Browne calls "an excellent potential for exercising a sort of negative power, a limited veto so to speak over how the white establishment uses its power."

Unlike too many black leaders, Mayor Hatcher is not a mere rhetorician but has a viable program which he has so far implemented with some success. Spearheading that implementation are the blacks who head fourteen of Gary's twenty-seven departments. This group includes newly appointed Police Chief Charles Boone whose 331-man police force now includes 100 blacks (old total: 40).

Hatcher has tried to make his administration democratic (small "d") by giving every member of the Gary community —especially the long-ignored blacks—some say-so in the city's workings. He subscribes to the principles suggested by his good friend, Georgia Representative Julian Bond in his discussion of a new black political movement. Bond explains:[2]

2. Julian Bond, "Practical Politician: Julian Bond," *The Black Politician*, vol. 1, no. 2 (October, 1969) , p. 28.

Epilogue

It must cast its votes in a unit. . . .

It must declare itself in the interests of laboring people, but not become the mistress of organized labor.

It has to seek out its natural allies in the Spanish-speaking community, but must not close its eyes to potential allies in middle class suburbia.

It must pay as much attention to a street light in a 50-foot alley as it does to national legislation involving millions of people, and international complications involving the future of the world.

It must maintain a militance and an aggressiveness that will earn it the respect of those it hopes to lead.

If there are any rules peculiar to this new movement in politics, they would be these:

1. That social, economic, educational, political and physical segregation and discrimination fill a very real need for the white majority;

2. That appeals to justice and fair play are outmoded and useless when power, financial gain and prestige are at stake;

3. That positions of segregation and discrimination will be adhered to until change is forced through coercion, threats, power or violence;

4. That initiative for black political education and organization must come from within the Negro community and must be sustained on a day-by-day basis;

5. That the geographical distribution of Negroes makes Negro-white coalitions desirable, but only when based on racial self-interest and genuine equality between the coalescing groups; but

6. That racial self-interest, race consciousness and racial solidarity must always be paramount in the deeds and words of the black political animal; when self-interest is forgotten, organized racism will continue to dominate and frustrate the best organized political actions of any political unit, and will leave it powerless and defenseless.

This new movement must address itself to solving America's white problem, to developing a new sophistication and consciousness in the black and white communities and in making democracy safe for the world.

If the 1960s was the decade of direct action and street re-
bellions against white racism, the 1970s can be the decade of
massive black political empowerment. For the organizing and
efficient use of the electoral process by the black community
is on the upsurge. It is quieter and less dramatic than the pro-
test politics of the 1960s. It is not, however, a less potent
weapon in the drive toward black liberation.

The significance of greater black political participation is
that winning office is only the first step toward political reconstruction. Without this political consciousness, blacks cannot transcend the realm of personality politics in which good
black men can be defeated by alliances between whites and
conservative blacks. Therefore, blacks are challenged not only
to put their fellow blacks in office but also to develop programs to change the political system and force it to be more
responsive to human need. Without that perspective, they
are doomed to continue taking "one step forward and two
steps backward."

Appendixes

MEMORANDUM FROM RICHARD GORDON HATCHER.

Subject: Federal Assistance to Gary. Review of Discussions in Washington on June 11 and 12, 1969.

The purposes of recent discussions between Gary city officials and key administrators from the federal government were twofold: one, to discuss the problems confronting the city, and the programs needed to act upon these problems; and two, to identify those federal resources which can be employed in Gary to meet the physical and social needs.

Throughout each discussion, one overriding factor was focused upon: the City of Gary is an urban microcosm: with a population of approximately 180,000, Gary suffers the classic ills of the nation's cities. However, it was emphasized that the *scale* of problems in Gary—while reflective of deep-seated urban problems generally—are yet small enough for innovative programs to make a real impact.

We asked, in essence, that HUD, HEW, OEO, and Labor regard Gary as an urban laboratory, and provide the city with the funds, technical assistance, and programmatic action necessary to change the ecology of the city.

Gary, with approximately 60 percent non-white and Latin American population is currently experiencing the alienation and polarization that exists between Black, Brown and White people. This Balkanisation of the races within the city affects all aspects of city life. As national attention is focused on whether multiracial political leadership can succeed, it is imperative that Gary be represented as a success. It is our basic assumption that through a federal-local partnership, Gary's efforts at comprehensive rehabilitation can be realized.

Other factors in support of using Gary as an experimental model are:

1. Inadequate housing—Experimental approaches would be welcomed in adding to the city's stock of low and middle income housing.
2. Need to change ecology of city—Gary's image presently is of a dispirited industrial community, beset by racial polarization, which needs to have its sights raised. Citizens and officials alike should be presented with higher goals to strive for, and some indication that it is not unrealistic to expect the achievement of these goals.
3. Resurgence of gang activity—Although perceived by many as a negative factor, many positives exist in the situation. The growth of gangs reflects in part the growing racial pride of many of Gary's youth. Some groups have indicated a willingness and desire for constructive activity; with proper programming, these young people could become a vital force for progress in the city.
4. Gary is operating on an inadequate revenue base—State law determines the taxing structure; the city cannot provide its citizens with needed services on what the states allows it. The city has shown in the past and is ready to do so again that it can make good use of technical assistance and cash grants furnished by the federal government and private foundations in filling some of the gaps in services and programs.
5. Reduction in crime rate—Police statistics indicate a gradual drop in the crime rate over the past six months. This is a heartening indication that recently instituted programs are making themselves felt. We see it as proof that currently existing problems are not immune to solution.

DEPARTMENT OF LABOR

Mr. Arnold Weber—Assistant Secretary of Labor (representing the Secretary); Mr. J. Nicholas Peet—Manpower Administrator; Mr. John Blake—Deputy Manpower Administrator; Mr. Merwyn Hans—Director of Programs; Mr. Lewis Nicolini—Regional Manpower Administrator; Mr. Leonard—Director of Intergovernmental Relations.

We indicated that the major problems and needs of Gary in the area of manpower were the following:

I. PROBLEMS

A. Unemployment among
  1. Females.
  2. Minority youth.

B. Paucity of entrepreneurial opportunities for minority group members.
C. Discrimination in building trades unions.
D. Inadequate transportation between low-income neighborhoods and regional employment opportunities.

II. Gaps in Manpower Training

A. Lack of upgrading programs.
B. Few training opportunities for white-collar jobs, retail sales, or service industries.
C. Lack of training of supervisory staffs which must deal with hard-core youth.
D. Non-existence of locally focused economic studies.
E. Weak summer youth-employment programs.
F. Confusion of state's role in manpower programs.

III. Program Needs

A. Greater emphasis upon and more resources for development of minority group entrepreneurial activities.
B. Overall economic study and analysis focused on:
   1. Attracting new industry.
   2. Creating new local support and supply industries to complement major local industries.
   3. Pinpointing specific training needs of youth and hard-core poor.
   4. Extrapolating data concerning Gary currently aggregated in metropolitan region data.
C. Federal attack on union discrimination.
D. Clarification of local alternatives in view of governor's veto of Work Incentive Program.
E. Training programs to fill existing gaps.

The following points summarize the discussion:
A. Concentrated Employment Program
   The Concentrated Employment Program will be refunded at approximately the same level as previously.
B. Inter-City Contractors
   Funds will not be released to Inter-City Contractors until they have reached a settlement with the Northwest Indiana Building Trade Council, AFL-CIO, which Mr. Hans thought would be soon. Mr.

Hans personally visited Hammond, and met with representatives from Inter-City and the Building Trades Council. The Gary team indicated apprehension that the Building Trades Council and representatives from the Department of Labor were not fully supporting the efforts of the Inter-City Contractors.

C. SOUL INC.

The Gary team requested that Soul Inc. be re-funded. Soul Inc. had initially been funded as a special impact project: however, subsequent administrative action placed it under E. and D. Mr. Peet stated that Soul Inc. had originally been funded by E. and D. funds. He asked Mr. Nicolini to check with Mr. Brandwine of the Department of Labor to determine if funds would be available for interim financing. Furthermore, it was suggested that the program could be funded by the OEO Special Impact program. All Department of Labor funds for Special Impact are being transferred to OEO, effective July 1, 1969.

D. HUMAN RESOURCES DEPARTMENT

The Assistant Secretary suggested that Gary's municipal system establish a Human Resources Department. Such a department would be the coordinating mechanism for all Department of Labor programs. It is envisioned that future funding will be carried out on a comprehensive or supermarket basis, with monies being earmarked for specific programs. Funds will flow from the Regional Manpower Administrator's office to the state and then to the cities. Funds designated for cities will receive a mandatory pass through the states. The initiative for all manpower programs must come from the cities and states and requests made to the Regional Manpower Administrator.

E. CAMPS

Modification of the existing CAMPS operation and establishment of new advisory groups are in the planning stages. These groups will function at the state and local levels relating to the governor and mayor respectively. Federal funds will be available for staffing local manpower advisory groups, thus insuring the development of centralized manpower capabilities.

F. JOB OPPORTUNITIES IN THE PUBLIC SECTOR

Projected in the president's budget is an allocation of fifty million dollars to provide for the upgrading of existing employees within City, State, and County governmental units. This program will also address itself to existing Civil Service and Grant-in-Aid programs.

G. INNER CITY RESIDENTIAL SKILLS CENTER

Mr. Nicolini reported that Gary had not been chosen as a site for the center. Such a center is planned for Chicago, but has not been finalized with the city administration. If such a center were to become operational in Chicago, Gary residents could participate. Mr. Nicolini is to follow up, and keep Gary officials informed of Chicago's progress in developing the site.

H. ECONOMIC ANALYSIS OF GARY

The Gary team indicated an economic analysis and labor survey of Gary is necessary. It was suggested by Mr. Nicolini that the parameters of such a study be explored with the State Bureau of Employment Security. He felt they might be able to provide the service. Mr. Peet provided a copy of a labor skill survey done in Oregon.

I. WORK INCENTIVE PROGRAM

The Gary team indicated concern that the governor vetoed the Work Incentive Program. It was indicated that the governor could not veto the program as it has been legislated by Congress. Mr. Hans stated that in the event the State of Indiana had not initiated the WIN program by July 1, 1969, the Secretary of Health, Education and Welfare has the option of withholding all State funds for public assistance or reallocating HEW funds provided for Indiana into the WIN program. It was suggested that since WIN is a manpower program and significantly affects Gary, that inquiry be made by the mayor's office to determine the status and method of implementation. The Employment Security Division is the prime sponsor in the WIN program. However, they cannot become operational until they have received a listing of eligible persons from the Department of Public Welfare, as the program is restricted to those persons on public assistance.

HOUSING AND URBAN DEVELOPMENT

Secretary George Romney; Mr. Floyd Hyde.
In discussions with the Secretary and Mr. Hyde, the following problems and needs were identified and discussed:

I. PROBLEMS

A. Housing Shortage. The mayor pointed out that no public housing was constructed in Gary between 1952 and 1968. Mayor Hatcher indicated that although a number of public housing programs have recently been initiated, the city is just "scratching the surface" and is not meeting the housing needs of the city. The Mayor pointed out that available land is a problem. Housing developments to the north are prohibited by steel mills and Lake Michigan to the east and west by corporate limits. He added that future growth is to the south, but this could require annexation. Presently vacant land on the west and far east sides of the city can be used for housing programs.

The Mayor in summing up stated that there is a shortage of low, moderate, and middle income housing.

B. Housing Relocation. The Mayor stated that the lack of relocation resources jeopardizes proposed urban renewal code enforcement programs, and public improvement projects. It was indicated that relocation is a key to all HUD housing programs, and that development or relocation resources should be related to demolition and urban renewal.

C. Urban Laboratory. The Mayor requested the Secretary to consider Gary as a site for HUD's experimental programs. The rationale would be that the city is large enough to have a multiplicity of urban problems, yet small enough to control projects and assess and evaluate their impact. Such an experiment will not entail prohibitive expenditures of funds.

D. Beautification and Environmental Improvement. The Secretary pointed out that Gary has a serious problem with air and water pollution. The Mayor indicated that a Beautification Commission has been established to deal with wide scale blight in the city. However, local resources are limited, and federal assistance is necessary.

E. Model Cities. Mr. Hyde stated Model Cities should emphasize "soft ware" programs (Human Services). He also felt that there should be emphasis on experimental housing and new towns. Mr. Staehle, Model Cities Director, indicated that this was in the planning stages.

F. Open Spaces. It was pointed out that Gary needed assistance in obtaining grants for Open Spaces Programs.

G. Racial Polarization. The Mayor noted that racial tensions affect the planning and construction of all housing programs in Gary. The Secretary commented that the unions made a positive response to Operation Breakthrough.

Following the Mayor's summation of Gary's problems, the Secretary said the Gary contingent should meet with HUD's assistant secretaries.

He requested Mr. Cox to arrange a luncheon meeting for the purpose of discussing technical aspects of Gary's housing needs.

The Secretary noted that funds for HUD programs were lodged at the regional level.

LUNCHEON MEETING

Mr. Sam Simmons—Assistant Secretary, Office of Equal Opportunity; Mr. Sam Jackson—Assistant Secretary, Metropolitan Development; Mr. Lawrence Cox—Assistant Secretary, Renewal and Housing Assistance Administration; Mr. Larry Finger—Assistant Secretary, Operation Breakthrough; Mr. William Ross—Acting Commissioner, Federal Housing Administration.

During the luncheon meeting, the following needs were identified:

II. NEEDS

A. Additional units of low income housing. Goal: Approximately 500 units per year for next decade.
B. Experimental and innovative programs to provide housing units at lower cost.
C. Additional units of moderate and middle income housing: Goal: Approximately 1,000 units per year for next decade.
D. New money programs to alleviate the high cost of housing financing.
E. Subsidy of experimental programs to develop new construction methods.
F. Interest subsidy funds for 1,500 units of Section 236 housing.
G. Approval of Model Cities program request for New Town-In-Town development.
H. Approval of Gary Housing Authority request for 1,000 units of public housing.
I. Funding for 200 units of Section 235 housing for stable families now residents of public housing.

III. In addition, the following issues were discussed:

A. Interim Financing. Mr. Ross was aware of problems caused in the construction of housing when interim financing was not available. He said interim financing for Gary's project could possibly be worked out through FHA and that he would investigate this possibility.
B. Technical Assistance. The Gary team requested technical assistance

for development of a Not for Profit Housing Corporation. Mr. Cox said he would have Miss Sybil Phillips assist Gary in developing such a corporation. Mr. Cox added that Richmond, Virginia and Pittsburgh, Pennsylvania have been successful in creating Housing Corporations. He suggested contacting Robbins Pharmaceutical and Mr. Gray in Richmond.

C. Public Housing. Mr. Cox noted that the Gary Housing Authority is requesting an allocation of 1,000 units and expects to erect this many units in approximately two years. Mr. Cox wondered if instead of having a set allocation of 1,000 units, why couldn't we use a program which would allocate a certain number of units for six months or some specified period of time and the Housing Authority would have to contract for constructing this housing within that period of time. This approach will be discussed with the Gary Housing Authority officials. Mr. Cox asked to be notified after the Common Council passed the resolution.

D. Water and Sewer Grants. Mr. Jackson asked if Gary had a program utilizing the federal assistance program for water and sewer facilities. It was explained that the Sanitary District of Gary currently has a program which is in the planning stage. The result of this planning will be a master plan for sanitary and storm sewers. The aim of the study is to determine where new sewers will be located, and to separate the existing combination sewers. The Sanitary District will follow up this planning period with an application to HUD For construction grants.

E. Advanced Land Acquisition. Mr. Jackson was asked if the program could be used to acquire the land for the Model Cities, New Town-in-Town experiment. It was generally felt that the purpose of this program is fairly well limited to public works and facilities. We will review our public facility proposals to see to what extent Gary can utilize this program.

F. Non-Cash Credit. Mr. Cox was asked if Gary could possibly use construction and planning funds for a Cultural Center as non-cash credits in its urban renewal program. Mr. Cox replied that funds in proportion to the use by an urban renewal area could be credited against the city's local share.

G. Operation Breakthrough. Mr. Finger was interested in the experimental housing element of Gary's Model City proposals. He asked what firms had been contacted and if we were recruiting other firms outside of the one mentioned. He said he would like to be kept abreast of our developments and felt that his program could be of great assistance to us. Mr. Jackson asked if our codes would allow us any flexibility in experimental housing and was informed that our codes are currently being revised and classes have been inserted to allow this experimentation.

H. 701 B Program. The Gary officials are to determine how this new program can best be utilized in Gary. The program should be tied into the Mayor's office to provide planning assistance to his office.

I. Section 236 housing. Gary's need for a reservation of 236 funds for 1,500 units for the next year was requested. It is stated that we currently have this many units being planned and expect the first applications submitted within the month of June. We are asking that this request be considered when funds are allocated for the State of Indiana.

J. Section 235 housing. Gary is requesting an allocation of 235 funds for the next year for 200 units to allow the stable families in Gary's six-family public housing units to purchase their homes. Mr. Cox felt this was not a priority item.

HEALTH, EDUCATION AND WELFARE

Mr. John G. Veneman—Under-Secretary; Mr. Mike Mahoney; Mr. Lee Lent; Mr. Jim Wirth.

The following problems and needs were identified in relation to HEW:

I. PROBLEMS

A. Lack of comprehensive, decentralized, accessible services in areas of health and social welfare.
   1. Lack of adequate structure for public and private service delivery.
   2. Lack of funds to design and implement programs for already identified needs.
B. Serious air and water pollution.
   1. Lack of local expertise to fully utilize available resources and implement strong local ordinance.
C. Family income supports.
   1. Numerous female heads of households.
   2. Extensive underemployment.

3. Uncertainty on status of proposed demonstration pilot project under Model Cities.

D. Vocational education deficiencies.
   1. High incidence of school dropouts.
   2. Universal industry needs for trained personnel.

E. Environmental health deficiencies.
   1. Serious rodent problems in midtown section of city.
   2. Lack of local programs and expertise.

F. Child development programs.
   1. High incidence of working mothers in marginal-wage jobs.
   2. Grossly inadequate programs of free and/or inexpensive day care.
   3. High incidence of Black and Latin poverty families whose children are unprepared to cope with public school curriculum in formative years.

G. Juvenile gang activity.
   1. Recent resurgence of hostile youth gangs in the city which aggravate crime and racial problems, compound racial polarization.

H. Mental health.
   1. Absence of adequate and/or inexpensive community mental health programs.
   2. Absence of facilities for community mental health programs.

I. Home management deficiencies.
   1. Several new programs of housing construction require preparation of low income families for increased skill in budgeting, management, and planning.

J. Latin community isolation.
   1. Bi-lingual education resources are virtually nonexistent for Mexican-American and Puerto Rican children.
   2. Weak community organization.
   3. Social welfare structure.

II. Needs

A. Approval and funding of pending Model Cities first year action program.

B. Technical assistance for:
   1. Design of comprehensive decentralized health and social service network.
   2. Strengthening local air and water pollution control programs and staff.

C. Designing adequate, modern vocational education program.
  1. Analysis and program development for work with resurgent youth gangs.
  2. Analysis and program development for community mental health services.

D. Funding for:
  1. Child care programs.
  2. Human services aide development.
  3. Rodent control.
  4. Training of environmental health inspectors.
  5. Bi-lingual education.
  6. Consumer education and protection program.
  7. Community mental health facilities and programs.

Discussions highlighted the following issues:

A. Income Maintenance.
  The Gary team indicated that the family allowance program planned for Gary was being held up by the governor's office. Before the program can begin in Gary, the governor must "sign off" or concur with the proposal. HEW officials agreed to speak with Mr. Kessler, the governor's administrative assistant, and seek concurrence from the state.

B. Comprehensive Health Plan.
  The need was stressed for HEW to follow up the study of Gary's Health Department carried out by regional HEW personnel by identifying and developing resources to create a comprehensive health plan for the city.
  The plan would include:
  1. Maternal and child health program. (This is being developed through Model Cities.)
  2. Environmental health programs: air and water pollution control, rodent control, removal of junked cars. The current air pollution control data is considered inadequate.
  3. Mental health component: Existing local facilities are completely outdated. Jails are often used to detain the mentally ill because other facilities are nonexistent. Few trained, competent staff people are currently available. A community mental health program

is proposed through Model Cities; however, greater support is needed.

4. Bi-lingual education facilities for Mexican-American children: an analysis of the Mexican-American community indicated the need for bi-lingual education for young children to make their school experience more meaningful and less threatening. Funds may be available through Title 7 of the Education Act. There is also a need for community education within the Mexican-American community.

5. Drug addiction program: HEW support is needed to expand a program proposed through Model Cities which will incorporate an existing but precariously financed program.

6. Child development program: social facilities for youngsters are nonexistent, with the exception of programs run by voluntary agencies, which do not meet community needs.

7. Home management program: monies are available through the Housing Assistance Administration.

Concerning the above-mentioned needs, the Under-Secretary commented that program monies were to go through the state. In cases where the state is not providing program support or money, the city should list the needs and submit them directly to HEW. He added that a memorandum be submitted to HEW that would identify programs that are needed by the city, but have not been developed by the state.

C. Follow Up.

It was suggested that Sid Gardner, Director for Center of Community Planning, would coordinate the follow up with HEW. It was further suggested that contact be made with M. H. Dumont, Director, Center for Community Studies.

A REVIEW OF THE HATCHER ADMINISTRATION, 1968-70. The following report has been extracted from a series of articles by George Crile III and is reprinted by arrangement with the *Gary Post Tribune*.

Richard Gordon Hatcher, age thirty-six, the city's first black mayor, one of the nation's most respected black leaders, and perhaps Gary's only nationally known figure, has had his share of troubles in the two and a half years he has been in office. He shares with other mayors the burden of answering to an impatient and aroused constituency for decades of neglect. All officials in public life are surrounded by controversy, but Gary's mayor seems to enjoy more than most.

Some say that the Hatcher administration has been successful because the city has not blown up, but many more complain that their garbage is not being picked up as efficiently as it should. Some say that Hatcher is the first honest mayor Gary has had in recent memory, but then he is charged with being an incompetent administrator. Some point to the millions of dollars of federal money that the mayor had induced into Gary, but others ask "Where is it?" Some hail him for bringing in talent from the outside, but most complain that he is turning his back on Gary's citizens in making his appointments. Some say he has improved Gary's image outside the city, but more allege that he spends all of his time out of town, and thinks only of his national reputation. Some say that the mayor has cracked down on organized crime, but almost all complain of increased street lawlessness. Some believe the mayor's sincerity when he says "For God's sake let's get ourselves together," but still others believe he wants to bring about a black revolution.

And the debate goes on.

It goes without saying that Hatcher has earned heated criticisms in certain areas. His performance has perhaps been poorest in the area of public relations. And this is peculiar because the achievements of the Hatcher administration are numerous.

Gary, it is often pointed out, is a microcosm of the United States. The center of the city has been dying in recent years. The national phenomenon of the flight to the suburbs is more noticeable here than elsewhere. Gary citizens „with sufficient capital have for years been exercizing their options and leaving the city. Simultaneously, in one of the great migrations of history, millions of unskilled and often uneducated Blacks and Latins have poured into northern cities in search of jobs. The city of Gary had a tax base that was not expanding, and an influx of new citizens that demanded greater public assistance, more government service, expanded educational facilities, low-income housing, rent supplements, and job training. These developments came at a time, as Councilman Eugene Kirkland pointed out, when "Gary has enjoyed bad government for over fifty years. The difference between Gary and Chicago," he said, "is that in Chicago, Daley wants 1 percent of everything. Here they always wanted 25 percent and that halted all business expansion."

When Hatcher came into office, the city faced an impending crisis as the era of black power had been ushered in, and city governments were being forced to become responsive to the long neglected needs of minority groups or face violent consequences. The times demanded that substantive programs be undertaken, and yet the city's shrinking budget was hard put, even to maintain the past level of performance. A retrogressive property tax was ill-equipped to add revenues.

The mayor realized that the conventional Gary approaches could not provide solutions to the city's problems. Jesse Bell, the present controller, explained "If we had wanted to be just another administration to steal money, we could have done that on our own. We would have just hired the local talent." But Hatcher sought assistance from new sources. He had already tapped the reservoir of talent in the surrounding universities. Urban affairs specialists from Indiana University's Northwest Campus, Purdue University, Calumet, and the University of Chicago had helped out in the campaign, and would continue to offer their assistance. When help was offered in the form of professional staffers from the Potomac Institute in Washington, and Kenneth Clark's Metropolitan Applied Research Center (MARC) in New York, Hatcher willingly accepted. A representative from the Labor Department came out to write up a proposal for Concentrated Employment Program (CEP) and the Democratic Presidential Administration offered whatever assistance it could. U.S. Steel responded to Hatcher's request for assistance with seventy thousand dollars to help pay the expenses of three top-level experts in the city administration. Later it would embark on a sizable housing project, a manpower development program, and even donate 145 acres of land to the city for the creation of a small boat harbor and park.

The early days of the Hatcher administration were marked by a rare spirit of cooperation as institutions from a variety of places sent help. The Ford Foundation and Gary's Committee of 100 were of particular assistance. Much of the help came because Hatcher was the country's first black mayor, but as Jim Gibson of the Potomac Institute explained, it was also because he was considered to be honest and a reform mayor.

Hatcher was seeking outside professional help—both for his permanent administrative staff and on a consulting basis, and this was a radical departure from traditional Gary politics, in which appointments had been made on a patronage basis and local people were almost exclusively chosen. As Indiana University's Frank Cizon explained, "Hatcher was moving on the principle of government by specialists rather than by political hacks. He is the beginning of a new breed of urban administrators that are thinking more of the future needs than the maintenance of the status quo." Cizon added that Hatcher had not always succeeded in finding specialists who were willing to take the jobs offered them, but at least he was trying. And he was not completely simon pure in staffing his administration, as at least two of his old supporters who possessed no special expertise were tapped for high posts.

Gary's city administrations have been seriously understaffed and underpaid. Previously, city employees could expect to bolster their salaries through unethical but time-honored practices. The mayor had allowed each department to run itself, with thirty-two separate departments reporting directly to him. No chain of command or general organization of city functions into spheres of interest had been worked out. Checks on performance were next to impossible, and some speculated that this was done on purpose to make it easier for corrupt practices to flourish.

Hatcher, working with the urban affairs specialists from the foundations and the universities, set to work on a plan for Gary that was based on professionalizing local government and bringing federally funded programs into the city. That effort is just now starting to bear fruit as the results of the federal program and the benefits of government reforms are surfacing.

Hatcher's predecessor, Mayor Katz, had started to win commitments for federal programs. But getting the commitments and seeing the money at work have not always been the same thing. The art of federal grantsmanship has a technology and set of rules all its own. Every city in the country is competing for limited funds and the mere process of submitting a proposal is an extraordinarily time-consuming process and guarantees nothing in return. Since Hatcher has been in office, the Katz-committed money has been released from the federal cupboard and put to work, and over eighty-six million dollars more of federal money has been committed to Gary. The impact of this cannot be appreciated until it is compared to the size of the annual city budget of about twelve million dollars! The mayor's frequent trips to Washington, though bitterly criticized in Gary, resulted in a working relationship with officials in the federal government that would be of great help in attracting federal programs into the city. He explained to cabinet members, and to key lower-ranking officials in both the Johnson and Nixon administrations, that Gary was ten years ahead of its time in the problems that it faces today—that there were over thirty cities in the country that would face approximately the same advanced state of decay, polarization, and pollution as Gary did then—and that the federal government had a rare opportunity to test out programs on Gary that might be successful elsewhere, later. Hatcher explained that Gary was small enough for the impact of federal government programs at available funding levels to be felt—that trying to test a program in a big city was as empty a gesture as throwing a pebble onto a beach.

It was this concept that Gary was the right-sized laboratory for federal programs, the mayor's talented salesmanship as well as his blackness, that won for Gary an unofficial designation as a priority city for federal programs. Hatcher's influence with both the Democratic and Republican administrations can be seen from the special status that Gary has retained in funding from the Department of Health, Education, and Welfare.

HEW originally received 193 applications from cities applying for the Model Cities Program. The decision to include Gary as one of the 50 Model Cities came after Hatcher's victory in the 1967 primary. Based on this decision, Gary received a planning grant. But HEW ran into budget cuts and could not follow through with funding for all of the designated Model Cities. Bob Ford, the regional director for Model Cities at HEW, explained that Gary was one of eight cities chosen for priority funding out of the twenty-four in this region. Hatcher's influence appeared to be the deciding factor in Gary's selection. This meant that millions of dollars of federal aid to the school city of Gary has come into Gary in the last two and a half years instead of being withheld as it has been in other cities.

With the rather sudden influx of tens of millions of dollars of federal programs into the city, the volume of work greatly increased. There were two cities to administer: one, the civil city with its traditional housekeeping functions, and the other the city of federally financed programs designed to serve more long range needs. The mayor was committed to continue to seek additional federal money and required, but didn't get, a separate staff to work on this project alone. As the new city administration moved ahead, it left in its wake a whole new set of administrative problems.

When Mayor Hatcher announced recently that he had brought over eighty-six million dollars of federally financed programs into Gary, few people were impressed. A precinct committeeman's reaction was typical: "He's been talking about federal money ever since he got into office, but I haven't seen any of it." One example goes a long way toward explaining how millions of dollars can be so hard to see.

The leased housing program financed by the Department of Housing and Urban Development (HUD) allows the city to use up to five hundred thousand dollars of federal money each year for the next ten years to subsidize rents for low income families. This represents a total commitment of five million dollars, and yet only about one hundred thousand dollars has already come into the city. It is confusing to a person looking for positive results for most of the programs are not of the "bricks and mortar" variety. The Model Cities Program, for example, has spent its money primarily in the area of health and education, and is only in its fourth month of full funding. METRO Corps, which administers the Office of Economic Opportunity's (OEO) antipoverty programs can't really be seen either. Yet the federal money already brought into Gary from these two programs alone is over four million dollars. The projected funding for Model Cities in Gary over the next nine years is twenty-six million dollars.

When Hatcher came into office he identified two problems that would be given priority treatment by his administration: to bring new low-to-moderate income housing into Gary; and to provide job-training and then jobs for the city's under-employed, unemployed, and hardcore unemployables. In one area—housing and urban development, the Hatcher administration has had a visible and dramatic success. A study of Gary's housing situation conducted by City Planning Associates of Mishawaka in 1967 reported that the condition of Gary's housing was critical: "No public issue is more serious in Gary today than the in-adequacy of housing," it maintained. Public housing programs have been in existence since 1937 and federal financing of low-to-moderate income housing since 1961, with the 221D-3 programs. But while other cities were using these programs, Gary had built no low-to-moderate income housing since the Korean War. To make matters worse, the existing supply of housing had been permitted to deteriorate to a level where 15 percent of all homes in Gary were deemed irretrievable and in need of replacement, and 25 percent in need of major repairs. Eighty-three percent of Gary's housing was in violation of some building code or other. The Building Department was severely criticized by the City Planning Associates report for not enforcing code regulations.

Within months of Hatcher coming into office, the Mid Town West urban renewal funds were freed, and the first phase of the seven-million-dollar project involving the tearing down of about three hundred dilapidated structures was completed. By the end of 1970, 3,432 new units of federally financed housing units representing over sixty million dollars, will have been completed, be under construction, or in the final planning stage. To date, only a small number of these houses are occupied, and the full effect has not been felt by many of Gary's citizens. A significant aspect of this new housing is its quality. Unlike earlier public housing, Gary's recent federal housing developments are not institutionalized in their appearance. The sites are scattered, the houses varied in design, of solid construction, and in general, an addition to the neighborhoods in which they are constructed.

The question of what it means to have sixty million dollars injected into the economy of Gary must also be given consideration. Most materials for local construction, over seventeen million dollars' worth to date, are purchased from Gary merchants. The workers that construct the houses are local residents. Over one thousand man-years of construction jobs and fifteen million dollars in on-site wages will result from the housing boom. Eventually, over 13,000 people who will be living in these houses will have their lives visibly altered. Further, if the housing construction continues at present rates, it will relieve over-crowding in other parts of the city, provide for price stability in the housing market, and help stop the alleged blockbusting practices of certain local real estate agents.

Hatcher set the seemingly impossible goal of bringing ten thousand new housing units into the Gary community in the next ten years, and so far the city is keeping up with this goal. Some of this housing would have been built whoever had been elected mayor because the 1967 housing legislation made housing projects much easier undertakings, but much of the credit must go to the Hatcher administration. Chuck Lazerwitz, the chief developer, explained why: "Hatcher has been more helpful than anyone else. He established housing as a priority for his administration and then set out to encourage all of us to get into the field. The Planning and Engineering departments at city hall have cooperated in full on many occasions, letters from the mayor to the Federal Housing Authority and the Housing and Urban Development people have freed money and broken up logjams."

Along with the building boom has come improved performance in the city's building department. In 1967, only 1,220 building permits were issued. Last year that number quadrupled, to 5,440. Building inspectors, who were renowned for their inactivity, have increased the number of inspections tenfold over an average year's total during the Katz administration. According to the City Planning Associate's study of Gary's housing in 1967, the building department was handling "only one-sixth of the case load that might have been expected of it." On the basis of the department's performance in 1966 and 1967 the study predicted that "it would require about thirty-two years to make but one investigation of each of the residential structures built before 1950. . . . Clearly, the growth of blight in Gary and the need of its people for safe and sanitary housing cannot abide this casual pace in code enforcement." Eighteen of the inspectors from the previous administration have resigned from the new department to date, and the overall number of inspectors has been increased. Despite more employees and higher overhead, the building department's expenses have been decreasing because of increased revenue from the permits.

The city is applying to the federal government for a concentrated code enforcement program, and has already started to use the lease (or rent) supplement program to induce home owners to put improvements into their homes. Under this program, the owner of a house is guaranteed that the city will rent his home as soon as it is brought up to code specifications. The city then rents the home out to a low-income family at a reduced rate, using the federal money to make up the difference.

This record has been compiled without the revenues from building permits paid for by U.S. Steel. For years, U.S. Steel merely decided how much money it owed the city for building permits and sent their money in in identical quarterly payments. In 1968 the Hatcher administration returned U.S. Steel's payment, refusing to go along with the traditional procedures. Negotiations have been underway since Hatcher came into office and an agreement is about to be announced which will result in considerably increased revenues to the city and an acknowledgment from U.S. Steel that they must abide by the laws of the city.

The second area where the mayor placed a high priority was in providing job training and jobs for the city's hardcore unemployables. Put bluntly, the goal was to take tax eaters and make tax producers out of them. To date about thirteen million dollars in federally funded manpower development programs are at work in the city. One of the chief problems in Gary's employment has been the lack of jobs for women without specialized skills. This is one of the areas in which the Concentrated Employment Program (CEP) is directed. Louis Nicolini, the regional director for the Labor Department which funds CEP, called Gary's program the "best and most successful of all" of the twenty-two CEP programs at work throughout this region of the country. Statistics in this area are often debatable, but the CEP program has already taken in 3,494 people and successfully placed 1,162 trainees in jobs. Over 1,000 more are presently in training. The Labor Department looks at its CEP program as an investment not unlike the GI Bill, which provided hundreds of thousands of veterans with the opportunity to get a college education. When all of the manpower programs are added up, the impact of taking thousands of previously unemployed or underemployed people, training them, and starting them on the road to self-sufficiency, is considerable. Criticism of Gary's CEP and other manpower development programs is widespread, the result of the sizable number of people who do not make it through the programs successfully, or who do not stay long in their jobs once placed. A certain percentage of failures was expected. The important figure to watch is the one that indicates the number of CEP graduates who remain in their jobs. Gary's CEP is doing well enough for the Labor Department to consider it a sound investment, worthy of refunding.

Other federal programs, though not as massive in scope, hold out considerable promise for Gary. In a general sense, these new programs have served to open the doors of opportunity to citizens who previously were shut out. All federally funded programs must be equal opportunity employers in order to qualify for funding.

Despite these encouraging statistics, the complaint is frequently lodged that the federal programs in Gary are aimed at serving the needs of the Black and Latin citizens exclusively, never those of the white population, and that this is unjust in light of the matching grants that all of Gary's citizens must pay to support these programs. These criticisms are without question valid, but the Hatcher administration cannot choose where it will spend the federal money committed to Gary. The available programs are designed almost exclusively for disadvantaged, low-income citizens. In Gary, these people are predominantly Black or Latin and the programs are carefully regulated by federal officials. Though most of the programs do not insist on matching grants, some do. But there is a loophole: charging the federal government rent for offices, typewriters, and other city equipment used, and for the services rendered by city employees in administering the given federal program. If this is not sufficient, there is yet another loophole: the city can take money out of one federal program without a matching grant requirement, in order to pay for another. The Model Cities money, in particular, can be used for this purpose.

Quite apart from these arguments is the benefit that comes to all Gary's citizens with the injection of close to a hundred million dollars of federal funds into the Gary economy. Sociologist Cizon pointed out the importance of the federal government as an employer and creator of new jobs in Gary. "The reason Gary hasn't been as hard hit as other cities by the recession is probably the federal participation which has taken up the slack."

There should be nothing unusual about a building department of a city which conducts valid building inspections, nor about a sewer system that disposes of sewage, nor of a competitive bidding process which is competitive. There shouldn't be, but in Gary there is. A few examples will serve to demonstrate how the Hatcher administration differs from its predecessors. At 26th and Cleveland, there is a large pumping station that was installed a number of years ago, but has never functioned. Len Coventry, the commissioner of the sanitary district, explained that it was built "to get votes for a politician." This would be hard to prove, but it is a fact that there are no sewers attached to it. A 2.5 million-dollar Rhode Island sewer line which is designed to allow water to run off into the lake in times of floods or storms is constructed below the Grand Calumet River. It is a relief sewer but the pipes are laid too low to allow the water to flow into the lake. In Glen Park, one of the city's largest pumping stations which cost two million dollars to build, is very rarely used. It was built for political reasons. Before Commissioner Coventry arrived in 1966, there were no engineers working in the sanitary district. "They didn't need one the way they worked," Coventry explained. "They gave out contracts on the basis of 'the wheel that squeaked the loudest politically got greased.' "

When Hatcher became mayor he was faced with a difficult decision. A five-million-dollar storm sewer line was scheduled to be constructed through mid-town Gary, where his political strength lay, and where he seemingly would owe primary allegiance. Coventry and the new city engineer Mahlon Plumb, explained that though the mid-town area badly needed storm sewers, the project was ill-conceived and would not work—that Gary desperately needed a master plan for sewers conducted by professional sanitary engineers so that money spent on improvements would not be washed down the drain as in previous administrations. In what Coventry termed a "courageous" move, Hatcher forced the two holdover Board members of the sanitary district to resign, encouraged the new board to abandon the five-million-dollar mid-town project, and to commission a master plan for sewers. This was done and the results showed that the sewer system was in even worse shape than had been thought. Some sewers were found to run uphill and thus only functioned during storms, when the pressure forced a flow. This construction is blamed for frequent flooding of basements in certain areas of the city. It was evidently cheaper to build a sewer pipe that ran uphill than to dig deep enough to allow it to continue to run downhill. Water was being shipped all the way around the city for delivery to a destination on the block where it started. Now the city has a master plan for sewers and whenever an addition or replacement is made, it is done according to the professional engineers' plan. The mid-town sewer line is included in the master plan and has a good chance of being built in such a manner that it will function.

When the Hatcher administration came into office in 1968, none of the files from the four boards which license contractors in Gary (General, Electrical, Sewer, and Plumbing) could be found, and yet written minutes of each meeting were supposedly taken. Minutes of these meetings are now kept and made available for the public to study.

Despite these substantial reforms and achievements in the traditional housekeeping functions of city hall, the Hatcher administration is faulted most severely in this very area. The performances of the General Services and Police departments are regularly called into question. These two departments have been handicapped to a certain extent. Councilman Eugene Carrabine, referring to the police department, observed "For a full year they have been hampered by the absence of equipment and manpower." The General Services Department was similarly hampered by lack of equipment. A proposed bond issue providing money for new equipment for these two departments was held up for almost a year. The money has just recently been released to purchase the badly needed equipment. The bond issue was submitted to the city council last June [1969]. Ordinarily, such issues pass through quickly. It was assumed that the equipment would be purchased and put to work by October. Instead, a citizen tax suit over a 1967 court case ate up several months, and then the council held the issue up for close to six more months. The state tax board then surprised everyone in an unprecedented and perhaps illegal move by eliminating two items from it. Councilman Eugene Kirkland and Paul Dudak were instrumental in this development. They flew to Indianapolis and personally requested provisions for the purchase of two helicopters be deleted. This was the first time in the history of the state of Indiana that the state tax board had cut an item from a bond issue. Consideration was given to challenging the act, but it would have meant added delays in getting the money released for the remainder of the bond issue.

By October, existing police cars were in critical condition. Patrolmen had to double up and the coverage of the city by patrol cars was considerably reduced. According to Bill Johnson, the city's safety director, crime is up 52 percent from March, 1969. The police force, which was substantially understaffed according to International Chiefs of Police statistics, was authorized to expand from 350 to 400, but recruits were hard to find.

The mayor, with only partial control over the police force, was not overly successful with his attempts at reform. He had received early acclaim for hiring an "honest" police chief, Jim Hilton, and for cracking down on organized crime. As was widely reported at the time, the visible end of organized crime left the city, setting up shop outside the city limits and going underground in Gary. But in time it became apparent that certain forces inside the police force were not sympathetic to the new chief, and Hilton's administrative experience appeared to be less than adequate to cope with the job. A new chief, Charles Boone, and the safety director, Bill Johnson, are launching new attempts at reorganization and reform, but no solution to the crime problem is on the horizon. Hatcher, although pointing to extenuating circumstances and to the failure of other cities in this regard, admits that the area of crime control is one of the failures of his administration.

The other department hard hit by the delay in passing the bond issue was the General Services department. Complaints of garbage not picked up on time, streets not being cleaned after snowstorms, and of the city dump burning have been numerous in the last two and a half years. In the beginning a large part of the problem was inexperience. The old hands that had been running the department for years were mostly fired, and the new ones often gained their experience at the public's expense. Drivers on garbage pick up runs and on snow plows did not always know their routes, and entire streets were, from time to time, missed. The problem was compounded by rundown equipment and the delay in getting new equipment into use. Gary's problem can be seen in perspective by comparison with Washington D.C. where the city's snow removal performance is a source of criticism. Washington has over twice as many miles of streets as Gary, but over two hundred pieces of snow plowing equipment to clear them. Gary has only twenty. At Gary's city dump, there are only four pieces of equipment, and all of these are in need of repair. None can be spared for the needed maintenance because the frequent fires force them to run from one crisis to the next. In fact, without the help of the men and equipment of the Marine Reserve, the city dump would be ablaze daily, and the streets of Miller would not be plowed after snowstorms.

It seems clear from all accounts that the general performance of the Hatcher administration in its first year in office suffered from inexperience. Jesse Bell, who was the only Hatcher aide to go through the campaign with the mayor and then join him in City Hall after the election, explained their dilemma upon walking into City Hall January 1, 1968; "Hatcher was an unknown councilman and lawyer. I was a physical education teacher. All of a sudden we were expected to run a city government." Bill Staehle, Model Cities director, observed that operations in the first several months verged on chaos. Local business and civic leaders who came to offer their assistance were left "cooling their heels" in the mayor's office for hours, often without getting to see him at all. Requests for Hatcher to speak and meet with government officials in Washington poured in. "In six months," Bell said, "we were two years behind and just how do you catch up?"

Fortunately, help came in the form of professional staffers from various foundations and governmental agencies. Jim Gibson, from the Potomac Institute in Washington, who stayed six months in Gary, and Carl Holman of the Urban Coalition were of particular assistance. Working with urban affairs specialists advising him, Hatcher started to reorganize the functioning of the operations at city hall. Thirty-two different heads of departments and programs were dealing directly with him, and yet he did not have time to see the people waiting in his outer office.

Bill Johnson the safety director recalled that the mayor's secretary for a long time simply "gave appointments to the first person to ask for one, rather than finding out if someone else could tend to the person's needs." City Hall officials complained that they could not get in to see the mayor when they needed decisions, often on routine matters, which under the existing system needed the mayor's approval. By October Hatcher recognized the need to reorganize his administration. In an exhausting three-day session at the Holiday Inn on Route 12-20, working under the supervision of a professional consulting firm, fourteen members of the mayor's cabinet exchanged criticisms, voiced their recommendations for reform and by the end of the session came up with a formal restructuring of the city administration. As a result, operations at city hall were divided into five general departments, headed by the mayor's three special assistants, and two members of the board of works. This had the effect of establishing spheres of interest and channels of communication that previously had not existed. Hatcher's secretaries learned to screen telephone calls and requests for appointments. They started to send people, whenever possible, to one of the five liaison heads. Hatcher was released for the first time from this unnecessary burden and from having to make constant low level decisions which could easily be handled by other people.

Perhaps most important in the long run was the establishment of a chain of command in which decisions could be made and in which not only department heads but division heads were responsible for the performance of their operations. In looking back, Controller Bell observed: "We've gained more experience in the last three years than the average administration could have in ten. The more problem solving you have to do, the better at it you get, and we've had a lot of problems."

Index

Index